TRANSFERENCE IN BRIEF PSYCHOTHERAPY

An Approach to the
Study of Psychoanalytic Process

TRANSFERENCE IN BRIEF PSYCHOTHERAPY

An Approach to the
Study of Psychoanalytic Process

Foreword by Charles Brenner, M.D.

Stanley Grand, Ph.D.
Joseph Rechetnick, Ph.D.
Dinko Podrug, M.D.
Elaine Schwager, Ph.D.

Department of Psychiatry,
Downstate Medical Center
Brooklyn, New York

 THE ANALYTIC PRESS
1985

Distributed by
LAWRENCE ERLBAUM ASSOCIATES, PUBLISHERS
Hillsdale, New Jersey   London

Distributed solely by

Lawrence Erlbaum Associates, Inc., Publishers
365 Broadway
Hillsdale, New Jersey 07642

Library of Congress Cataloging in Publication Data
Main entry under title:

Transference in brief psychotherapy.

   Bibliography: p.
   1. Psychotherapy, Brief.   2. Transference (Psychology)
3. Psychotherapist and patient.   I. Grand, Stanley.
RC480.55.T7   1985   616.89'14   84-24422
ISBN 0-88163-033-0

Printed in the United States of America
10   9   8   7   6   5   4   3   2   1

Contents

Foreword

This monograph is the first fruit of a research project that the authors have planned and executed over a period of years. The central focus of the project is transference: the aspect of the relationship between patient and psychotherapist that is determined by wishes and conflicts originating in childhood. Its aim is twofold: first, to test the therapeutic value of focusing on transference in short-term psychotherapy conducted on a weekly basis and, second, to study the development of transference in such a therapeutic setting in order to add to current knowledge of transference as it develops and is dealt with in the setting of psychoanalysis when practised *lege artis*.

The authors have brought to their task a high degree of psychological sophistication, much clinical experience, and a wealth of scholarship. Thus one of the features of the book is an extensive, critical review of the recent literature dealing with transference in psychoanalytically informed, short-term psychotherapy. Its chief value, however, lies in the thorough documentation of the clinical basis on which the authors' conclusions are based, and in the promise the work holds for progress in understanding the origins and development of transference in the psychoanalytic situation.

The authors are to be congratulated on their first volume. The ones to follow will be eagerly awaited.

New York, N.Y.   Charles Brenner, M.D.

1

Introduction

Despite Freud's (1926, 1933) repeated expressions of skepticism regarding the possibilities of shortening the arduous task of therapeutic analysis, efforts in this direction have appeared with a cyclical regularity over the past 60 or so years (Alexander & French, 1946; Davanloo, 1978; Deutch & Murphy, 1955; Farenczi & Rank, 1925; Malan, 1976; Mann, 1973; Sifneos, 1972; Stekel, 1940). Each new cresting of the wave of short-term psychotherapy has roused strong controversy and widely diverging opinions from proponents and opponents about the genuineness of reported effects, as well as critical efforts on the part of theoreticians to expand our clinical conceptualizations in order to accommodate the reported successes by such therapies (Winokur, Messer, & Schact, 1981).

Historically, the failure of these short-term therapies to take hold as recognized modes of psychotherapeutic intervention has been due to complex factors, including, but not completely explainable by: (1) a general skepticism about the reported successes, particularly with respect to the durability of therapeutic effects; (2) adverse clinical experience among "second-generation" advocates of the treatment approach, leading to a loss of enthusiasm (Malan, 1963) and a cycling down of therapeutic effectiveness; (3) a lack of agreement in the field at large as to what constitutes therapeutic effectiveness; and (4) general confusion with respect to what specific component processes of the short-term treatment are responsible for change in psychological functioning. While the latter factor is a perplexing problem for the field of psychotherapy at large, its impact on brief psychotherapy is magnified

1

greatly because of the intrinsically active stance required by these treatment approaches and the necessity for rapid interventions.

Currently, we are experiencing yet another resurgence of interest in short-term treatments, with proponents claiming astounding rates of "complete cure" among those patients selected for treatment, for example, 88% in Davanloo's (1978) sample of 130 patients treated over the past 15 years at Montreal General Hospital. Success rates such as these have been skeptically received, even among those (Wallerstein, 1966, 1979) more favorably disposed toward the clinical and theoretical yield of carefully documented studies of brief psychotherapy (Malan, 1963, 1976). Indeed, Wallerstein (1983) has characterized Davanloo's (1978) work in this area as an "evangelical statement of a movement, persuasive only through its charisma" (p. 784).

It is not without some trepidation, then, that psychoanalytic clinicians approach brief psychotherapy for the purpose of research. Given the evangelic nature of the current movement, and the seemingly inherent difficulties in establishing the clinical efficacy of brief psychotherapy, it is little wonder that this has been so. Fortunately, however, clinical efficacy is not the only focus for research in this field. From the perspective of the psychoanalytic researcher interested in exploring the nature of the therapeutic process, there may yet be something of real interest and value in the brief psychotherapy model, despite the ambiguities that exist regarding the clinical efficacy of such treatments. What we have in mind here is that the brief psychotherapy model could provide the psychoanalytic researcher with a laboratory for studying processes difficult to explore in the more traditional approaches. Thus, despite the skepticism about brief psychotherapy as a treatment of choice, its value as a research tool is still largely unexplored. To the extent that a short-term treatment mirrors, or could be made to mirror in telescopic fashion, processes analogous to those mobilized in traditional psychoanalytic psychotherapy, the short-term treatment model could provide a context for the study of those process variables. It is our intention, in this monograph, to explore such possibilities.

The study of process variables in more traditional long-term treatment approaches is replete with problems well-known to the psychoanalytic researcher. Process research requires the study of a complete event; anyone attempting to study the psychotherapy event is immediately besieged with the enormous problem deriving simply from the lengthy time period required to complete this event. In addition, the researcher is confronted with overwhelming data generated during the course of this event. Even if one is willing to await the conclusion of the event, the necessity for data reduction via the selection of target sessions or, in the extreme, microscopic analysis of selected samples of text from one or a number of sessions from the long analysis of a single analysand (Dahl, 1972, 1974) seems to lose the richness of the process and can only answer special types of research questions at best. If one wishes to study those processes intrinsic to psychological change in treatment, then what is required, at least, is that the complete event of the treatment be available. Despite its purported limitations, brief psychotherapy does meet this requirement.

There are, of course, other requirements for the study of process, but these have to do with the particular process that the researcher defines for study. For example, if one is interested in the relationship between transference and therapeutic change, as in the present case, then it is a requirement of the treatment approach that it does indeed enable a transference to develop and that this process itself can be shown to change during the course of the treatment event. Further, if one is interested in relating the data to more traditional conceptions of the clinical phenomena of transference, then it is also required that management of the developing transference be akin to its management in the more traditional approach, that is, via timely and tactful interpretation rather than manipulation of the treatment relationship (Brenner, 1976, 1979).

It is with respect to this last point that complications arise regarding the usefulness of the brief psychotherapy model for the study of transference. Several researchers in this field have developed brief treatment approaches that attempt transference interpretations both rapidly and toward specific transference contents. For example, Mann (1973) uses a technique of rapid interpretation of transference wishes based on the patient's early associations around issues of separation, whereas Sifneos (1979) also makes early interpretations, but limits these specifically to Oedipal issues. Both the rapidity of the interpretive work and its predetermined focus raise important issues concerning the development of an analyzable transference. Granting that the appropriate timing of an interpretive intervention is always a subjective decision, and that brief psychotherapy is a telescoped process ranging anywhere from 1 to 40 or so sessions, one does expect more rapid and active management of transference issues here than in long-term psychoanalytic work. However, it is a hallmark of the classical analytic stance that transference be allowed to intensify and coalesce into a repetition of elaborated early prototypic relationship struggles (i.e., emerge as a transference paradigm). From our point of view, early interpretation of transference reactions would certainly modify such developments. Despite Gill's (1982) recent advocacy of early in-

(over)

terpretation of the transference in the "here and now," it is our view that, for transference to evolve in brief psychotherapy in a way that mirrors its development in the more traditional approach, it would be necessary to await the development of a positive transference (i.e., alliance) and limit interpretive work to that aspect of the treatment relationship which becomes meaningfully organized as a transference resistance.[1] This issue will be discussed more fully in subsequent chapters of this monograph, but suffice it to say that, from our point of view, there is the danger in brief psychotherapy and elsewhere that focusing too early on the prototypic relationship, while intensifying the patient's awareness of the transference, may also encourage intellectual and other defenses against the working through or resolution of the transference.

With respect to the issue of focus, the predetermination of specific issues toward which interpretive work is directed is contrary to the more classical approach, which allows patients wide latitude in arriving at their own focus. The imposition of focus on the part of the therapist is a manipulative technique as contrasted with the nondirective approach of long-term classical analytic treatment. While short-term approaches generally do require the imposition of focus, an analytically derived short-term treatment would minimize this imposition by allowing the focus to emerge from the patient's own associative flow. In our view, this characteristic of allowing the focus to emerge from the patient's associative flow is intrinsically related to the evolution of the transference paradigm. From this perspective, the manipulation of the focus in most short-term treatments is synonymous with the manipulation of the transference paradigm and results in a decidedly nonanalytic stance to the dynamics of the treatment situation. The study of transference in brief psychotherapy must take account of this issue as well. We will return to a fuller discussion of this problem in subsequent chapters of this monograph.

These, then, are some of the characteristics of the brief psychotherapy procedures used in this study of the relationships between transference and therapeutic change. More formally stated, the treatment utilized in this study is a form of brief, transference-

---

[1]This is not to say that we disagree with Gill's position insofar as it relates to the early interpretation of the transferences of defense in the here and now. What we do question, however, is the tendency in brief psychotherapies to make rapid interpretations of such transferences as projections or displacements onto the analyst of reactions originally directed toward childhood prototypes. It seems to us that for such interpretations to be experienced by patients in an affectively meaningful and mutative way, they must occur within the context of an organized transference paradigm.

focused, psychoanalytically oriented psychotherapy. This approach entails the early relatively nonfocused attention to transference themes emerging from the natural flow of the patient's initial statement of his problems. As the therapy progresses, the patient's attention is selectively focused on one or two critical transference themes as these emerge in the unconscious conflictual transference manifestations in the evolving treatment situation. The positive transference is fostered during the initial phase of the treatment, with the patient being encouraged to express feelings toward the therapist. As treatment progresses, these feelings are related to significant figures, represented in both genetic and extratransferential conflicts. Later in the treatment, as negative attitudes and separation themes emerge, the transference is now interpreted to help the patient understand those attitudes and their origin in early childhood experiences. Overall, the focus of the treatment derives from those conflicts that have been brought into the treatment situation via their unconscious transference manifestations. Once manifest, these transference issues are systematically interpreted by the therapist to facilitate the process of working through.

It is almost inevitable that the reader would, after reading this "programmatic" passage, be hard put to explain how this approach would practically differ from Mann's, Sifneos's or Davanloo's. They would certainly claim as insistently that they do not force prefabricated, procrustean formulations on the patient, and that they are as nondirective as possible. Obviously, the core issue is how to choose a focus in a short-term treatment in such a way that it is neither arrived at so late as to render its working through ineffectual nor so early as to preempt and distort a more encompassing formulation of the conflict. How does the therapist evade the Scylla of passivity and the Charybdis of suggestive, premature formulations? In planning this work, we were not intending to pose this question, since our own focus was directed elsewhere, that is, to establish the usefulness of "complete event" analogues for the study of the classical analytic process. Yet, we were repeatedly forced to deal with this question. Although we do not present a comprehensive answer, we believe we offer a demonstration of how a more "neutral" approach, which becomes progressively focused as it hones in on the developing transference dynamics, is a way truly to maximize the therapeutic potential of the short-term therapy.

This monograph will be devoted to the study of one patient, treated by this specific psychoanalytically oriented form of short-term, transference-focused psychotherapy, and for whom follow-up data are available. Our purpose here will be to trace the development of transference and whatever structural reorganization can be established to have occurred over the course of treatment, and to evaluate the stability of these changes following treatment. First, we will define our specific clinical-research methodology and provide a clinical-research rationale for this methodology; we will then turn to the literature on brief psychotherapy in order to evaluate the role of transference in this sort of work. Then we will provide an overall summary of the case, and describe the compromises and conflicts reactivated in this patient, and whatever specific reorganization has occurred during this treatment via clinical summaries and comments on the work over its entire course. The results of pre- and post-psychological testing with a standard clinical battery of tests will then be presented as converging data for the evaluation of clinical change. We will also present the data from our first follow-up testing of this patient 8 months after termination of treatment in order to evaluate the stability of treatment effects during the first year. Thus the present study will attempt to trace the nature and stability of whatever psychological reorganization has occurred in our patient as a result of this short-term treatment and will do so by providing the reader with as comprehensive a description of the course of the clinical work as is possible within the obvious constraints of written text.

There are several reasons for presenting our case material in so much detail. For one, we believe there is too little clinical data available in the psychotherapy and psychoanalytic literature for use in correlating treatment phenomena with theoretical concepts. Theoretical progress in this field is accomplished not only through the formulation of new all-encompassing or part theories, but mainly through subtle changes that occur in the meanings of key psychoanalytic concepts that accrue primarily through clinical experience in the consultation room. Thus, from a clinical perspective, there is a flexibility and elasticity in psychoanalytic concepts, which allows new insights to be incorporated into our theory without requiring that we recreate the whole theory anew with each subtle shift in our clinical experience with the meanings of our key concepts (Sandler, 1983). Such flexibility, however, is often also a liability. It is a major reason why psychoanalysts often have difficulty agreeing on or even arguing about a theoretical point, and why it takes so long for a novice to become proficient in theoretical understanding. There is the constant danger that our theoretical concepts may become too vague and confusing because of their elasticity. It is this danger which makes it not only important, but necessary constantly to link these concepts to clinical data. Thus, by presenting our case in so much detail, we are attempting to "reference" the theoretical concept of transference to the clinical data at hand. This is especially important for the field of short-term psychotherapy, where too many "old" concepts are being given new and expanded meanings which are at once confusing and conducive to unintended ambiguities.

There is yet another reason for presenting our clinical material in so much detail. Our central concerns in this study are, first, to demonstrate that transference "exists," i.e., that the concept can be meaningfully inferred from and related to the session transcripts and, second, that by enabling the reader to follow the emergence and handling of the transference in a session-by-session sequence, we provide the most informative vantage point for understanding this case and a number of attendant technical and theoretical issues in dynamically oriented, short-term psychotherapy. It therefore seemed logical to present as much of our data base as possible to ensure that the reader will understand what we mean by the inferences and generalizations we make about this case as well as about short-term treatment generally. Furthermore, by providing so much clinical data, we enable the reader to form as independent an understanding of the case as is possible from a written text. We have no illusions that the reader can ever be fully independent in his judgment of a case, even when provided with a completely verbatim transcript. After all, the therapist in this case always chose but one of many possible interventions, and each reader subsequently must deal with the dialectic unity of his personal vision and the patient's narrative. Indeed, reading the narrative transcripts of this case enabled both the therapist and the other members of our research team to see various aspects of the case differently than the therapist had originally seen them in the treatment session itself. Further, there were even differences in understanding from one reading of the case material to another. Thus, by providing the reader with so much clinical material, we hope to provide some basis for evaluating our own clinical and theoretical conclusions.

Finally, it was our expectation that the reader might feel the need for different levels of exposure to the clinical data base. We therefore provide this exposure at three levels of complexity: first, we present an overall summary of the case; second, we present a summary of each individual session, with the verbatim transcript of the most incisive moments in each session presented so as to give the reader abundant examples of both the patient's style and the therapist's mode of intervention; and third, we present comments on each session in which various themes are traced and trends are pointed out. In this way, the reader will be able to follow our inferences and generalizations as they became clear to us in the treatment process.

2

Research Strategy: Issues and Assumptions

A basic problem for all clinical process research is the identification of those dimensions that are relevant and have crucial significance for the process itself. The identification of such dimensions always entails a selection from a number of possible dimensions which may also be relevant, but which may not be central to the clinical work. Usually, the selection of crucial dimensions rests heavily on the theoretical orientation of the clinician (Wallerstein, 1963), but often it is based on the clinician's own clinical experience or that of his colleagues. Through repeated contact in the actual clinical situation, conviction usually develops over time about the relevance and crucial significance of particular dimensions of the clinical interaction. This conviction becomes organized around conceptual schema congruent with the clinician's theoretical orientation, and these schema then serve to make understandable the many diverse and often enigmatic aspects of the clinical process. Through the organizations afforded by such conceptual schema, the clinical data become compelling for the clinician with respect to validating the reality of the dimensions in question.

For researchers who approach the clinician's data from the "outside," however, the clinician's conviction has the appearance of an unexamined assumption. Clinical researchers, operating under methodological constraints with respect to accepting the clinician's conviction at face value, must establish their own sense that the crucial dimension in question actually exists. They need to develop their own conviction about the reality of the dimension in question prior to studying the way this dimension operates in the clinical situation. Researchers must establish for themselves that the dimension of interest is compelling, real, and actually identifiable in the clinical data, and they must do this through the use of their own methods, approaching the data from the position of the outside observer.

From this perspective, then, we are led to a particular approach to clinical research in which we clearly divide the undertaking into two discrete phases: a first phase of establishing the clinical reality of the process of interest, and a second phase of experimentation proper.

In the initial phase of establishing the clinical reality of the process of interest, the primary task for researchers is the development of a sense of conviction that the process exists and can be identified in the clinical data. In this phase, the researcher proceeds much like the clinician does in developing a sense of conviction: the researcher becomes immersed in the clinical data to the point that the process in question becomes compelling, real, and identifiable for him. Using his own conceptual and theoretical understanding of the process, the researcher begins to identify examples of the process in the clinical material at hand. If he is successful in doing this, others can be enlisted in the process in order to validate his growing conviction. As a final step in this phase of the research, the researcher attempts to establish links between the process of interest and other data sources, extending the validity of his own conviction through convergences with data drawn from sources other than the clinical situation itself. Having achieved all of this, the clinical researcher is now ready to enter the second phase of research—the phase of experimental research proper.

Experimental research proper begins with the operationalization of the process of interest. This step is necessary in order to make the process quantifiable, repeatable, and public. It is only at this stage that experimentation can begin. Having operationalized the process, the researcher can now begin the study of the covariation of the process of interest and other variables in order to reveal relationships that can define the generality of the process. It is in this phase that hypotheses are tested and predictions either confirmed or rejected.

In the present monograph, we shall be focusing on the first phase of clinical research—that is, the effort to establish the clinical reality of the process of transference as it manifests itself in a short-term, psychoanalytically oriented psychotherapy. Our goal is to develop a sense of clinical conviction that a process we deem to be important to the meaningful reorganization of an individual's experience in psychoanalysis can be traced over the course of a relatively brief psychotherapeutic treatment. Our research approach, which we shall detail below, is a quasi-experimental approach since our goal is that of attaining clinical conviction. At this stage of research, we believe formal validation is not only unnecessary, but may even impede the course of the work.

RESEARCH APPROACH

As a first approximation to establishing the clinical reality of the process of transference, a case selected for treatment was audio-recorded and played for a member of the clinical-research team following each session. The therapist and the clinical researcher discussed the significant issues and dynamics appearing in each session and planned specific interventions for the following session. This procedure was followed throughout the 14 weeks of treatment as a way of maintaining a check on what actually was done and said by the therapist, as well as establishing a strategy of interventions that had some consensus.

A third member of the research team who was essentially blind to the nature of the patient's specific complaints and dynamics was enlisted to test the patient at the outset and conclusion of the treatment, and to provide follow-up testing 8 months after the completion of treatment. A standard clinical battery was used, including Wechsler Adult Intelligence Scale, Rorschach, Thematic Appreciation Test, Bender Gestalt, Figure Drawings, and some additional tests of interest to this third team member that will not be reported here. In addition, the patient was given a battery of paper-and-pencil tests of the "stress response" developed by Horowitz (1977, 1979), which the patient completed at the outset and conclusion of his treatment. These data will be reported in a subsequent publication.

Finally, a fourth member of the research team was asked to listen to all of the audio-recorded sessions and to write clinical process formulations for each session, consisting of what he thought the major dynamic themes were and how they were being played out in the transference. Subsequently, all four members of the clinical research team met to discuss their findings and a consensus was obtained regarding the quality of the developing transference and the extent of its structural reorganization during the treatment course.

One final aspect of our research approach was to select a patient who was experiencing a current life stress of major dynamic significance in order to ensure meaningful participation in the treatment situation. A decision was made to focus on a life-threatening event. We established contact with the director[1] of the Cardiac Rehabilitation Program at

---

[1] We wish to express our appreciation to Dr. Richard Stein for his participation in screening suitable patients for this research.

Downstate Medical Center, who then offered the brief psychotherapy program to his cardiac patients as an adjunct to physical rehabilitation training following their heart attack. Volunteers from this program were screened for their potential to utilize a verbal form of treatment and their willingness to participate on a regular basis for the length of the treatment course.

THE CLINICAL REALITY OF TRANSFERENCE

When we speak of our goal of establishing the clinical reality of transference, what do we mean? The clinical reality of a process variable is given by its identifiable systematic variation over the course of treatment. With respect to the transference, this means that the researcher can point to the way transference emerges in the treatment, intensifies, and then subsides as therapeutic effort is brought to bear on it (i.e., as it is worked through). A condition for this goal of the first phase of the research is, therefore, that clinicians can detect and identify aspects of the clinical interaction that they informally agree on as representations of transference, and they can do this with some sense of clinical conviction. Thus the first step in identifying transference in this phase of the study of brief psychoanalytic psychotherapy is to establish a working definition of transference that is generally agreeable to clinicians and broad enough to encompass the phenomena of interest. By transference, we mean the displacement or projection of the patient's feelings, attitudes, reactions, or thoughts that properly belong to significant figures of the past, onto the analyst. In our study, we want to show that transference, as we have defined it, does indeed occur, intensify and subside in properly conducted brief psychotherapy, and that this process can be sufficiently well identified by clinicians so that a sense of conviction about its course emerges.

Two methods are available for establishing clinical conviction that transference has occurred, and some sense that it has undergone systematic variation during the course of the psychotherapeutic treatment. One method entails informal, intuitive agreement by a group of clinicians that a particular process has occurred; the second method relies on extra psychotherapeutic data, which dovetails with the clinical process. The first is the method of group consensus; the second, the method of converging data.

These methods require that certain conditions be met by the clinical research approach. The method of group consensus requires that clinicians evaluating the clinical data all share a common theoretical orientation toward the process under study. Seitz (1966) has already shown how divergences in theoretical orientation interfere with group consensus in ratings of clinical material. He suggested that this interference can be significantly reduced, simply by focusing all raters on the same level of the phenomenon to be rated. In our study, all clinicians shared a "classic" psychoanalytic orientation toward the data and presumably could all target the same level of the clinical material.

The method of converging data requires a data source which taps the same or similar levels of the phenomena under scrutiny as does the clinical interaction. Since our definition of transference calls for a process that entails projective or displacement mechanisms, the converging data should also entail the same or similar mechanisms. Our choice for a converging data source was, then, the data deriving from projective tests. Here, also, the patient projects or displaces feelings, attitudes, reactions, or thoughts properly belonging to significant figures of the past, onto the figures and inkblots of the test materials. To the extent that the mechanisms are similar, data deriving from these data sources should provide convergences with the clinical material and do so at a level similar to the level targeted in that material.

There are several additional and perhaps even more important requirements, however, that a study of transference in brief psychotherapy must meet. First, the form of treatment itself must allow transference to occur. Although it is true that transference is a ubiquitous phenomenon (Bird, 1972; Brenner, 1976, 1982), which will occur whether or not the treatment approach encourages it, it is also true that most forms of brief psychotherapy discourage its intensification. The assumption of most brief psychotherapies is that transference entails a regressive process. As such, it must be actively confronted and limited in intensity in order for treatment to be effectively terminated within the time limits of short-term work.

However, if one wishes to study transference as it is manifest in psychoanalysis, then the treatment form must allow transference to emerge in a similar way to the way it occurs in psychoanalysis. Thus it must allow transference to emerge spontaneously, intensify, and coalesce into a focal struggle with the analyst, that is, it must activate a new version of the original core conflict. Our goal here is not so much to demonstrate the efficacy of such a process, as contrasted with other forms of brief psychotherapy, but to make possible an opportunity to study this process in as close to its intended meaning as possible.

A second requirement for the study of transference is that the treatment form must encompass a complete event. Process studies must permit the initiation, development, and termination of the process in question. The treatment must be studied as a whole so that the natural form of the process in question may emerge. No matter how short, the treatment must reveal a definable opening phase, middle phase, and end phase. Given this requirement, the form of treatment must be time-limited with a specified end point—that is, a form that establishes a frame within which a complete process may unfold. In this, both the therapist and patient would be expected to experience the treatment as a complete event.

We undertook a form of brief time-limited psychotherapy which could be distinguished from most other forms of brief psychotherapy with respect to the therapist's stance toward the analytic work. The therapeutic stance of the present treatment could be characterized as neutral vis-à-vis the more active therapeutic stance of most other brief psychotherapies. Again, the issue here is not one of therapeutic efficacy, but rather one of attempting to remain as close to the classic model as would be possible considering the exigencies and therapeutic requirements of the particular patient being treated.

From our perspective, the essence of a neutral therapeutic stance, as opposed to an active stance, lies in the therapist's ability to remain in a position equidistant (A. Freud, 1954) from id, ego, and superego—that is, midway between wish and prohibition.[2] In this position, the therapist refrains from any active manipulation of transference wishes and simply provides the patient with empathic understanding. Thus, as Freud suggested (1913):

> to insure (the patient's collaboration) nothing must be done but to give him time. If one exhibits a serious interest in him, carefully clearing away the resistances that crop up at the beginning and avoids making certain mistakes, he will of himself form such an attachment and link the doctor up with one of the imagos of the people by whom he was accustomed to be treated with affection (p. 139).

The kinds of mistakes Freud had in mind here were given a little further on in the following quote:

> It is certainly possible to forfeit this first success (i.e., the positive transference) if from the start one takes up any standpoint other than one of sympathetic understanding such as a moralizing one, or if one behaves like a representative or advocate of some contending party. . . (p. 140).

The essence, then, of Freud's stance in psychoanalysis was decidedly opposed to the active manipulation of transference wishes. In the treatment form utilized here, we strove to maintain compliance with

---

[2] A fuller discussion of the concept of analytic neutrality will be presented in Chapter 7.

Freud's technical advice on the management of transference. Since the neutral and empathic stance of the therapist appears to facilitate the early development of the positive transference, and the positive transference is, as Freud (1912) suggested, the "vehicle for success in psychoanalysis" (p. 105), our treatment approach aims to facilitate the early development of the positive transference. As in classical analysis, we would expect that the consistent frustration of the patient's wish for transference gratifications will ultimately lead to the emergence of negative transference imagos and, in necessarily reduced and limited fashion, a gradual transformation of the therapeutic relationship into a new version of the patient's core conflict, that is, a transference neurosis. The interpretation of these negative imagos as they appear in the form of resistances to the continuation of the treatment constitutes the phase of working through those aspects of the transference neuroses mobilized in the brief treatment. Finally, as the end of treatment rapidly approaches, the working through of separation issues heralds the end phase of treatment. In all this, the form of the brief treatment mirrors the form of the classic analytic treatment, even though telescoped in microscopic fashion by the imposition of time limits.

A brief contrasting of the active stance vis-à-vis the transference may be helpful in distinguishing the essential features of our approach. The essence of the active therapeutic stance lies in the early interpretation of underlying wishes vis-à-vis the therapist. By bringing the unconscious fantasies, or imagos, rapidly into consciousness, the active stance limits the gradual emergence and intensification of transference reactions. It also limits the natural development of a core conflictual focus, which essentially defines the transference neurosis, on behalf of a predetermined focus which the *therapist* deems to be crucial. Thus the active stance, by rapidly interpreting toward oedipal or separation issues, actually manipulates the transference in the predetermined direction established by the therapist, and essentially sidesteps the patient's natural regressive movement toward the transference neurosis. More seriously, however, the active manipulation of the transference enhances a subtle and unexamined transference reaction in the patient consisting of the patient's early imago of an omnipotent and powerful parental figure. Whether such imagos are also enhanced, as countertransference problems in the therapist, is an as yet unexplored matter. In the next chapter, we will review the literature on the subject of transference in the brief psychotherapies in order to shed some light on these largely unexplored issues.

3 The Analysis of Transference in Brief Psychotherapy

It is a matter of common agreement among dynamic psychotherapists that transference is, as Freud (1925) suggested, at the heart of psychoanalytic work. The centrality of transference is as much a matter of concern for those engaged in the brief dynamic psychotherapies as it is for those engaged in more classical long-term work. However, while traditional psychoanalytic psychotherapies view transference as the major dynamism powering the analytic work, and its analysis the aim of such work, brief psychotherapies propose a number of innovations with respect to the technical management of transference which distinguish their treatment aims from those of the classical psychoanalytic approach. Basic differences exist between the way transference is managed in psychoanalysis and its management in the brief dynamic psychotherapies, and those differences reflect the distinctive aims of these different treatment forms. Since work with the transference in the present case was designed to fit more closely with the aims inherent in the traditional approach to the management of the transference, discussion of the distinctive features of the analysis of transference in the brief dynamic psychotherapies will be helpful in setting the framework for our own work, as well as providing an opportunity to comment on the utility of a neutral, non-directive form of brief psychotherapy as a research tool for the study of process in psychoanalysis. Thus the purpose of the present chapter is to summarize the issues posed by the major approaches to the management of transference in brief dynamic psychotherapies, and to contrast these brief approaches with the more traditional approach studied here.

BASIC ISSUES

It has been suggested (Winokur, Messer, & Schacht, 1981) that brief dynamic psychotherapies, because they utilize the major techniques of interpretation, clarification, and confrontation of the patient's anxieties, defenses, and impulses in connection with current, past, and transferential relationships, present "a formidable challenge to long-term analytic therapists" (p. 127). They pose this challenge because the brief therapies "claim substantial improvement in a short time without compromising the values embodied in orthodox psychoanalytic technique" (p. 127). Apart from the purported clinical efficacy of short-term treatment, there are two theoretico-clinical issues that are raised by such an assertion. First, the fact that the techniques of interpretation, clarification, and confrontation of the patient's relationships are utilized by the brief psychotherapies is not, in and of itself, evidence that the values embodied in orthodox treatment are not compromised by this approach. The psychoanalytic use of such techniques always occurs within a specific context—the psychoanalytic situation (Stone, 1961)—a context so different from that of the brief psychotherapies that one might question whether the techniques themselves might not take on a meaning quite different from their meaning within the classical context. As we shall show below, the parameters of time-limit, focus, and early intervention create conditions for treatment very different from traditional conditions and exert influence on the patient of possibly far different import than do the classical techniques that they utilize.

The second issue raised by the above assertion concerns a distinction between transference as a theoretical construct and transference as a technical problem. The adherence to theoretical principles and the technique for so doing in the clinical situation represent two very different domains of discourse. All brief dynamic psychotherapies concur on the fact of transference as a theoretical construct underlying the dynamics of the therapeutic relationship. The classical psychoanalytic approach to the transference, however, implies a very specific technical stance, that is, neutrality, with respect to its analysis. Despite the inherent difficulties that surround the concept of neutrality and the controversies that these difficulties have produced with regard to our understanding of the analytic relationship[1] (Gill, 1982, Stone, 1961), the tools of psychoanalytic technique are utilized basically within such

---

[1] A number of important issues in the current debate over the importance of "real" versus transferential aspects of the analytic situation stem from the failure to distinguish "neutrality" from the "abstinence principle." This problem will be discussed in Chapter 7.

a technical framework rather than one that is essentially manipulative. Thus, although agreement may exist about the centrality of transference as a theoretical concept, there is little basis for agreement with regard to issues concerning the technical management and analysis of the transference in brief psychotherapy and psychoanalysis. Thus from the perspectives of both therapeutic context and therapeutic stance, most brief treatment approaches reflect radical departures from the values embodied in more orthodox analytic technique.

HISTORICAL PERSPECTIVE: THE BASIC PARAMETERS OF BRIEF PSYCHOTHERAPIES

Despite the frequently reported claim that Freud was the first brief psychotherapist (Marmor, 1980; Rogawski, 1982), his own view on innovative techniques for shortening treatment was decidedly negative. In 1926, Freud said, "I am unfortunately obliged to tell you that every effort to hasten analytic treatment appreciably has hitherto failed. The best way of shortening it seems to be to carry it out according to the rules" (p. 224). Again, in 1933, Freud cautioned against innovative techniques:

> The therapeutic ambition of some of my adherents has made the greatest efforts to overcome these obstacles so that every sort of neurotic disorder might be curable by psychoanalysis. They have endeavored to compress the work of analysis into a shorter duration, to intensify transference so that it may be able to overcome any resistance, to unite other forms of influence with it so as to compel a cure. These efforts are certainly praiseworthy, but, in my opinion, vain. They bring with them, too, a danger of being oneself forced away from analysis and drawn into a boundless course of experimentation (p. 153.)

It is toward this latter danger, of being forced away from analysis and its specific values, that we think Freud's major objection was directed. According to Freud (1913), innovations that artificially alter the course of analytic treatment interfere with the natural development of the transference. Since a central concern of analytic work is the analytic resolution of the constriction of early prototypic relationship conflicts, interference with the development of transference represents a radical shift away from the central values inherent in the analytic process. Let us turn, then, to the major parameters of brief dynamic psychotherapy in order to consider in what ways they may interfere with the natural development of a classical psychoanalytic process.

The earliest germs of a brief psychotherapy movement occurred in the "active" therapeutic work of Ferenczi (1950), who, through actively indulging or prohibiting impulsive expressions of his patients, hoped to shorten the arduous task of analyses which were becoming interminable, insofar as this issue was understood in the early 1900s. By establishing himself as a loving parent substitute through hugging, kissing, and fondling his patients, he hoped to repair the damage caused by ineffective and traumatizing actual parenting.

This active and manipulative technique was subsequently further elaborated in the book by Ferenczi and Rank (1925), detailing their efforts to shorten psychoanalysis through a more focused concern with the patient's current relationships and an emphasis on affective experiential factors in the treatment process. In addition to their emphasis on focused current relationships and affective experience, these authors established the parameter of time-limit as an explicit principle of short-term technique. Thus, Ferenczi and Rank had already established, as early as 1925, several of the main parameters of brief psychotherapy as it is known today. Their emphasis on focus, current relationships, and time-limit defined the essentials of a technique designed to limit regression and undercut the development of the transference neurosis.

Although Ferenczi subsequently abandoned such concrete efforts to manipulate the transference, residues of this parameter still appear in more subtle and less concrete forms in the techniques of current brief psychotherapies. Thus the intention to direct and manage the affective relationship with the therapist, when elevated to the status of a technical precept, contrasts sharply with analytic principles which encourage self-determination and individuation. Since the evocation and working through of early prototypic relationship themes and conflicts is a central aspect of the psychoanalytic process, approaches which limit these developments not only clash forcefully with psychoanalytic principles, but aim for the establishment of quite different treatment goals as well. Indeed, the effort to shape behavior through the establishment of a new affective relationship with the therapist actually defines most brief psychotherapies as fundamentally behavioristic in their treatment orientation.

With respect to the fixed time-limit, although Freud (1918) himself had used this innovation in his work with the Wolf-Man, he viewed this as an expedient, or in Eissler's (1953) terms, a parameter of the treatment. Freud (1937), generally took a dim view of this strategey, as suggested by the following comment on Rank's work:

> We have not heard much about what the implications of Rank's plan has done for cases of sickness. Probably not more than if the fire brigade, called to deal with a house that had been set on fire by an overturned oil-lamp, contented themselves with removing the lamp from the room in which the

blaze had started. No doubt considerable shortening of the brigade's activity would be effected by this means (pp. 216–217).

As a parameter of treatment, the time-limit would, according to Eissler (1953), need to be analyzed and its effects worked through prior to the termination of treatment. Elevated to the level of a technical precept, not requiring analysis, it becomes a potent extraanalytical force in the treatment, the effects of which are only partially understood in current brief psychotherapy work (Mann 1973).

Perhaps the most influential of the earlier proponents of the briefer treatment approaches was Franz Alexander. He and French (1946) were most explicit in the formulation of a treatment approach that was distinctly manipulative with respect to the transference. Alexander and French suggested that in all cases in which the transference relationship is consciously controlled and directed, and in which the therapy embraces both transferential and extratransferential situations, progress tends to be more rapid, to require fewer sessions, and to maintain a higher emotional participation on the part of the patient than is true in cases treated by the older method of effecting a complete transference neurosis. Thus the power of the therapist lies in his management of the transference relationship in order to bring about a "corrective emotional experience".

Central to the techniques advocated by Alexander and French is the limitation of regression in the treatment situation. Varying the frequency of sessions, interrupting the treatment, presenting early transference interpretations, and using the chair instead of the couch were techniques used to minimize the tendency to regression in the therapy. By limiting regression, these authors attempted to prevent the gratification inherent in the patient's dependency on the analyst. Limiting the development of the patient's dependency supposedly facilitates awareness of this need and mobilizes the patient to express it verbally in the treatment situation.

In a similar vein, it has been assumed by current brief psychotherapists that the psychoanalytic context for treatment, which encourages regression, increases dependency to a point that is unmanageable, given the limited time frame of brief treatment approaches. Furthermore, it has been claimed that the evocation of a transference neurosis is actually inimical to the therapy since it fosters a passive infantility in the patient, which conflicts with the goals of the brief treatment approach (Davanloo, 1978). Despite these assertions there is little evidence to show that a technique which encourages regression and the development of a transference neurosis is inimical to the goals of brief psychotherapy. Indeed, without such evidence might we not assume that a brief psychotherapy embodying the context and stance of a psychoanalytic treatment may be as effective in attaining short-term therapeutic goals as the antiregressive techniques of current brief psychotherapies claim to be. While such a possibility has not yet been formally studied, Malan's (1963) approach, which we will discuss below, is suggestive in this regard.

Although the corrective emotional experience has not been an explicit part of current brief dynamic psychotherapies, the active and directive stance vis-à-vis the transference has remained a central feature of this work. Although most current brief psychotherapists seem to reject the idea that their work provides a corrective emotional experience for the patient, they seem not to consider the fact that the active and manipulative character of the treatment situation does result in a particular sort of induced therapist–patient relationship. This, in turn, does create a situation in which both partners to the dialogue are forced into specific and predefined roles with respect to one another and results in the emergence of specific transference fantasies. By not viewing these developments analytically, brief psychotherapists often fail to explore the meanings that are stimulated in their patients by the therapeutic stance itself. For example activity on the part of the therapist with respect to early and deep interpretive work could result in specific fantasies in which the therapist becomes an omnipotent, powerful, and almost magical figure by dint of his early recognition of deep aspects of the patient's personality which are far beyond what the patient can consciously recognize alone. On the other hand, there is the further danger that the therapist may come to believe in his or her own power to "read" the patient's unconscious from minimal cues. This may result in significant countertransference problems.

The traditional approach to understanding deep levels of the patient's dynamics and discovering the original prototypic relationship models was given by Freud (1916–1917), who suggested that once

> the treatment has obtained mastery over the patient, what happens is that the whole of his illness's new production is concentrated upon a single point—his relation to the doctor. . . . When the transference has risen to this significance, work upon the patient's memories retreats far into the background (p. 444).

It is this perspective on transference that forms the basis for a more classical understanding of the curative factors in psychoanalysis. Through the demonstration that the transference repetition is a form of remembering, the patient gains a sense of conviction "that what appears to be a reality is in fact only a reflection of a forgotten past" (p. 19). Further, Freud (1940) suggested that "a patient never forgets again what he has experienced in the form of transference; it carries a greater force of conviction than anything he can acquire in other ways" (p. 177).

The centrality which Freud assigned to this factor of remembering via the transference repetition places all forms of treatment that press for the elimination of regressive repetitive transferential acting *in* the treatment situation at some distance from the psychoanalytic model for psychotherapy. Early interpretation of the transference and explicit manipulative techniques for minimizing the transference regression all operate to reduce the intensity of the repetitive remembering and the sense of conviction that goes with it. From this perspective, the oft-quoted criticism that psychoanalysis, as an interpretive technique, limits affective reaction in favor of intellectual insight, seems to be a reversal of the true state of affairs. By attempting to eliminate regression, the brief psychotherapies appear to be closer to this position than does psychoanalysis. Gill (1982) has recently emphasized the distinction between resistance to the awareness of the transference and resistance to the resolution of the transference. Essentially, this distinction cautions us that simply helping a patient overcome the resistance to become aware that reactions are misplaced is no guarantee that the patient will be able to give up such reactions in the future. Overcoming the resistance to the resolution of the transference entails the arduous task of working through the transference neurosis. Thus the first task of the analytic work aims at helping the patient recognize that current interpersonal conflicts are, in actuality, intrapsychic conflicts. The ability to effect this transformation depends in part on the patient's capacity to relinquish partially the defensive hold on reality, that is, on the capacity for controlled regression. Thus therapies that technically interfere with analytic regression also interfere with the process of effecting this transformation. If this transformation does not occur, it seems unlikely that the patient will overcome resistance to giving up repetitive acting in the transference, that is, resistance to resolving the transference. It would appear, then, that by limiting the regression and avoiding the transference neurosis,[2] the brief psychotherapies direct their therapeutic efforts toward resolving the

---

[2]Despite Brenner's (1982) recent criticism that the concept "transference neurosis" is an "anachronism" and involves a "tautology" insofar as it is indistinguishable from a neurotic symptom, in our own view, there is still some usefulness in distinguishing circumscribed transference reactions from the more encompassing expressions of transference in which "the whole of [the patient's] illness's new production is concentrated upon a single point—his relation to the doctor" (Freud, 1916–1917, p. 444). From this perspective, our conception of the evolving of the transference neurosis entails the organization of a major prototypic relationship theme played out in relation to the current object (i.e., the analyst).

resistance to the awareness of the transference, while minimizing therapeutic efforts to resolve the resistance to the resolution of the transference.[3] In this sense, the brief psychotherapies seem to focus more attention on intellectual awareness than affective working through.

This, however, is not what contemporary brief dynamic therapies claim. Indeed, all current brief psychotherapies operate within a framework of transference interpretation, which takes account of what Malan (1976) has called the triangle of impulse-anxiety-defense—that is, the same framework within which classical analysis operates. Thus the claim of brief psychotherapies is that they, along with their long-term analytic colleagues, clarify and interpret patterns of impulse-anxiety-defense by linking past, present, and transferential relationships, and do so in what is claimed to be an affectively meaningful way.

---

[3] We are using the distinction between the two types of resistance to transference interpretations in a somewhat different sense from Gill's (1982) recent usage. For Gill, resistance to the awareness of transference entails the patient's unwillingness to recognize feelings held toward the analyst per se, whereas resistance to the resolution of the transference entails the patient's unwillingness to recognize that feelings and attitudes toward the analyst are indeed misplaced from earlier prototypic relationship struggles. The two sorts of interpretations are sequential and in tandem insofar as interpretations of the resistance to the awareness of transference precede interpretations of the resistance to resolving the transference. The sense that we wish to give the distinction between these two types of transference interpretations is that the former type of interpretation allows the patient to experience, more directly, feelings toward the analyst which then become available for the repetitive reenactment of the earlier prototypic relationship paradigm. In this sense, interpretation of the resistance to the awareness of transference encourages regression toward the transference neurosis, which will then be the subject of interpretation of the resistance to resolving the transference. To the extent, then, that brief psychotherapies (as well as the therapies modeled on Melanie Klein's object relations school) make deep interpretations of the original prototypic relationship struggles immediately on the initiation of treatment, they are attempting to resolve the transference by bypassing the important work of preparing the patient to accept, with emotional conviction, that such transference actually exists. In this sense, we suggest that their deep interpretations are, in actuality and paradoxically, only directed toward resolving resistance to the awareness of the transference; without the emotional conviction that transference is actually operative, it is hard to see how such deep interpretations could be meaningfully integrated and worked through.

Clearly, the distinction we are making here has implications not only for analytic technique, but for the divergent theoretical models that underlie the major types of psychoanalytic treatment currently available (e.g., those based on a developmental model, entailing a reestablishment and correction of the early vicissitudes in the structuralization of the mental apparatus and those based on the model of intrapsychic conflict, entailing the working through of repeated cycles of regression and fixation). This distinction also has implications for issues concerning the value of introjection versus identification in the amelioration of psychopathology in the therapeutic process. These issues, however, go far beyond the scope of the present monograph.

However, we have already argued that the context within which clarification, interpretation, and confrontation is done, and the therapeutic stance by which it is effected in brief psyotherapy, is so different from the context and stance of the traditional analytic situation that it is perhaps misleading to consider these techniques to be equivalent to those used in traditional work. Brief psychotherapies, by establishing the parameters of time-limit, focus, and active technique, are essentially manipulative rather than "neutral" with respect to the therapeutic work. Although brief psychotherapies may utilize the basic techniques of psychoanalysis, the modifications of the typical long-term context and analytic stance make comparisons with the work of psychoanalysis difficult at best and misleading at worst.

CURRENT BRIEF PSYCHOTHERAPIES AND THE TECHNIQUES FOR MANAGING THE TRANSFERENCE

Having considered several important issues generated by the basic parameters of the brief psychotherapies, we will now turn to a more focused consideration of the techniques for managing the transference in some of the recent, more prominent approaches to short-term dynamic psychotherapy. If short-term approaches are to be useful for the study of psychoanalytic process variables, they would have to provide a more traditional context for treatment which employs the kind of neutral analytic stance characteristic of the classical approach. Addressing the current techniques for managing the transference utilized by brief psychotherapists should highlight the distinction we are making between a directive approach and one which is neutral.

Winokur et al. (1981) have clearly articulated the basic technique of current brief psychotherapists as one which utilizes rapid and forceful juxtaposition of genetic and concurrent events with transference interpretation in order to avoid repetitive acting in the transference. They state:

> Instead of waiting for the genetic links to emerge gradually . . . following a transference interpretation, in STDP [Short-Term Dynamic Psychotherapy] the therapist forcefully presses the patient to make these links and actively aids in the process by offering a generous number of reconstructions of his own. This rapid juxtaposition of the genetic material with the transference interpretation ensures that the feelings that emerge do not remain directed at the therapist. The requisites for mutative interpretations of high immediacy and real affect are realized without disruptive effects. In this way, the patient's feelings toward the therapist are not allowed to develop into a crystallized attitude [transference neurosis], and

the disorientation and regression that sometimes follow transference interpretation in psychoanalysis are avoided (p. 133).[4]

Of the current group of brief psychotherapists, both Davanloo (1978)
and Sifneos (1979) are probably the most vigorous in their adherence
to the principles articulated by Winokur et al. For example, Sifneos
accepts only highly motivated patients whose core conflict presumably
is at the oedipal level. For these highly motivated patients, Sifneos
uses a technique of vigorous anxiety-provoking confrontation of the
patient's defenses against oedipal wishes. Flegenheimer (1982) has
described Sifneos' technique in the following way:

> The most common example [of Sifneos' technique] is the direct attack on the
> patient's defenses rather than attempts at interpreting the meaning or
> function of the defenses. Other aspects of the patient's production or be-
> havior may be challenged directly, sometimes in what seems to be a mock-
> ing or sarcastic manner. Thus, when a patient strays from the [oedipal]
> focus, when he or she avoids or disagrees with an interpretation, or when
> there is a general slack in the flow of material, the therapist is likely to
> confront the patient in a direct, forceful, challenging way (p. 65).

This forceful and sometimes belittling approach by the therapist is
designed to prevent the emergence of pregenital issues and to compel
patients to understand their symptoms and struggles as a product of
oedipal conflicts.

Similarly, Davanloo (1978) is relentless in his confrontation of his
patients around issues of anger and aggression. Although he does not
engage in the sort of provocative challenging that Sifneos does, he
does present himself as a strong, and somewhat authoritarian figure.
The manipulative elements in his approach are clearly seen in an excerpt reported by Winokur et al. (1981): [Davanloo, after coming 30
minutes late for a session, questioned the patient's denial of any anger:]

---

[4]This quote poses as many questions for the reader as it answers. Without attempting
to analyze the implications of Winokur et al.'s summary statement of the technique of
brief psychotherapy comprehensively, we would simply raise the question of what it
means that "the therapist forcefully presses the patient to make these links and actively
aids in the process by offering a generous number of reconstructions of his own." It
seems obvious to us that the therapist, by proffering a generous number of his own
reconstructions to an admittedly pressured patient, runs the very serious risk of distort-
ing not only what the patient is able to remember of his own personal life history, but
steers the associative process in such a way as to fulfill the therapist's own prophecy. The
theorizing on short-term therapy too often fails to address this paradox. In the absence
of adequate theoretical clarity on these issues, one is reminded of Freud's early technique (1895) of pressing patients' foreheads and insisting they remember the trauma.
This was, of course, before Freud (1905) had "discovered" the transference.

"You say the therapy is important to you . . . and yet you say you don't mind if I come half an hour late"; and later, "Isn't it you fear the retaliation . . . that I won't want to continue to see you?" The patient gradually admitted his transferential fears and, before he had time to consolidate these into an established attitude, the therapist suggested that the same problem existed with the patient's boss. A few minutes later, in the same session, the patient recalled a dramatic retaliatory act by his father when he was a young child. Davanloo then assured the patient that he no longer needed to fear his father's retaliation (p. 133).

It is not clear, from the excerpt, whether Davanloo's lateness was, itself, part of the intended intervention. However, the fact of the lateness already bespeaks a cavalier, manipulative attitude on the part of the therapist, in the absence of any exploration of the patient's feelings about it. Rather, Davanloo proceeds with forceful confrontation of the patient's resistance, which is gradually expanded to both his current relationship with his boss and ultimately to his fear of retaliation from his father when the patient was a young child. To round the picture off, Davanloo then returns to the patient's current experience by reassuring him that he no longer needed to fear his father's retaliation. Presumably, this latter reassuring stance is now internalized on the basis of Davanloo's authority. If, indeed, internalization does occur, one might consider the alternative interpretation that it reflects an identification with a new aggressor (i.e., Davanloo) rather than an internalization of a new attitude toward an old aggressor.[5]

Given the constraint of time limitation and the goal of meaningful structural reorganization, brief psychotherapists feel required to make early, deep interpretations and to make these forcefully. However, pressing the patient to make genetic linkages on the basis of "generous reconstructions" by the therapist can result in strong feelings toward the therapist that are both outside as well as inside the transference relationship. Thus, forceful and perhaps fanciful reconstruction may intensify distrust and anger, or dependency and helplessness, with respect to the therapist as a real person rather than only as a transference distortion. This is not to say that such techniques may not occasionally be clinically useful and, perhaps in some cases, helpful. But the use of such techniques moves the treatment away from a neutral analytic stance that facilitates remembering via repeating, and toward

---

[5] How likely this unwanted alternative does occur is well-illustrated by what the author of a very complimentary and enthusiastic article in the New York Times Sunday Magazine on Dr. Davanloo and his group intended as an example of a successful therapy: on a follow-up appointment, a year following treatment, an ex-patient exclaims, while viewing the tape of one of her sessions, how "incredibly masochistic" she was and how she would much rather be "sadistic." (Sobel, 1982) Apparently, the understanding that she no longer needed to react masochistically was obtained by transforming her reactions into their sadistic counterpart.

the manipulative stance discussed earlier in which the therapist takes on the role of omnipotent, powerful, magical person. The rapid juxtaposition of genetic and concurrent events with transference interpretation does not ensure, therefore, that feelings that emerge can be directed away from the therapist, but instead may create feelings directed toward the therapist which are not only repetitions of the prototypic relationship struggles for which the patient came for help.

For example, consider Davanloo's intervention reassuring the patient that he no longer needed to fear his father's retaliation. Might not such an intervention have been based on a disavowal of Davanloo's unconscious apprehension of his own anger at the patient and his own fear that he has pushed the patient too far. The force and challenge of the interpretive style of both of these brief psychotherapists is more than likely responsible for a whole gamut of feelings in the patients that may or may not have anything to do with chronic transferential feelings indicative of the prototypic relationship struggle. Thus to say that rapid and forceful juxtaposition of genetic and concurrent events with transference interpretation does not allow feelings toward the therapist to crystallize is not, strictly speaking, an accurate appraisal of the actual state of affairs. More likely, it stimulates feelings and attitudes that are linked directly to what the therapist is doing, and it may artificially maximize an attitude in the patient based more on the therapist's assumptions of what troubles the patient than on what actually is central to the patient's own experience. Although high immediacy and real affect are quite likely generated by this approach, it is not so clear that these feelings are accurate reflections of early prototypic relationship conflicts and themes intrinsic to the patient's pathology.

Winokur et al. (1981) suggest that the reassurances and authoritative pronouncements on the part of short-term therapists be considered part of the technical stance of actively encouraging neutral self-observation, and actively disconfirming the patient's view of the therapist. Apparently, statements such as "Let's look at . . . [the problems] so that we can learn something. . . . Don't run away" (p. 134), or "If you put me, however, in the position of authority . . . then you are making me something that I am not" (p. 134) are designed to encourage the patient to participate as an equal partner in the therapy and to prevent regression. Such statements, however, lean heavily on the establishment of influence through authoritarian and forceful attitudes on the part of the therapist. Whether the effects of such techniques are due to the "isolation of a critical ego" or are the result of a regressive passive acceptance of the therapist's authority is not yet clear in the cases reported in the brief psychotherapy literature. Indeed the active, forceful, and directive qualities of brief psychotherapies appear to color the therapeutic alliance in ways which are certainly antithetical to the neutral stance of the psychoanalytic approach.

Of the current group of brief psychotherapists, both Mann (1973) and Malan (1963, 1976) are probably the least vigorous in their efforts to confront forcefully their patients' resistance to link genetic and concurrent events with the transference. In addition, both assume a therapeutic stance closer to the classically neutral stance than others in this field.

For Mann (1973), time assumes an important place in his treatment approach, consistent with his view of its unconscious meaning in the lives of therapists and patients. The developmental progression from a sense of infinite timelessness to finite times, with its recognition of separation and termination, forms the basis for his theory and technique of time-limited brief psychotherapy. Mann believes that the distinct limitation of time, the selection of a central issue or a conscious focus that is particularly cogent for the unconscious life of the patient, the therapist's confidence that he or she can achieve therapeutic gain in a short period of time, and the known termination date all serve to fuse objects, past fantasies, and conflicts in a telescoped manner and invest the therapist with an intense positive transference very quickly. Although Mann's interpretive technique is never as forcefully confrontational as the technique utilized by Davanloo and Sifneos, and interpretations are not targeted toward very deep levels, he does consider the establishment of therapeutic focus as essential. Mann accomplishes this by actively focusing on the central issue agreed on with the patient in the early sessions. To the extent that Mann's approach holds specific assumptions about universal prototypic relationship conflicts, his active, manipulative stance runs the risk of imposing such conflicts on the patient whether or not they are salient for the patient at a particular time. Freud (1937) cautioned against waking sleeping dogs, but apparently Mann's approach attempts to do just this. He states, for example, that although expressions of the basic conflicts may vary according to the social, economic, and cultural background of the patient, the conflicts remain the same for any and all patients. These are: (1) independence versus dependence, (2) activity versus passivity, (3) adequate self-esteem, and (4) unresolved or delayed grief. He states that each of the four basic universal conflicts expresses varying degrees of the capacity to tolerate and manage effectively object loss. They are also so closely related to each other that all four may be clearly detected emerging in the course of treatment.

With these orienting assumptions, Mann actively pursues and directs the transference in order to obtain the reactions he assumes must be present. Thus Mann says that what are felt to be relevant details in the history are repeated often as a way of suggesting, impressing, and teaching the patient. Furthermore, he uses the transference relationship in a similarly directive way. For example, in the fifth interview, he supports the patient when he tells her, "you are making progress," and later actively attempts to induce negative transference reactions by saying, "you are allowed to be angry about me too." In the 10th interview, Mann asks the patient directly, "Do you think you will miss me?" He tries to elicit transference feelings from the patient by asking her if she has any feelings about the idea of finishing and not coming anymore. In all of this, the patient does not give direct responses to Mann's questions. In the 12th session, Mann asks the patient a number of times if she likes him and will miss him but, again, does not succeed in eliciting direct reactions. Finally, at the end of the last session, Mann responds to a question the patient asks about what she will do if something bothers her and she can't face it, by telling her, "I think you can face it and will be able to."

It is clear that while Mann is not as forceful or aggressive in his active confrontations of patients, he does direct the transference toward obtaining reactions that he has determined should be present, even though the patient may not be aware of these reactions nor understand them as transference manifestations. While such active efforts undoubtedly influence the resistance to the awareness of transference issues around the conflicts Mann assumes to be operative, it is not so clear in which way these efforts influence the resistance to the resolution of the transference.

Of the current group of brief psychotherapists, Malan's (1963, 1976) approach probably comes closest to the classical stance with respect to the technical management of the transference situation. Contrary to Davanloo and Sifneos, Malan does not engage in the kind of forceful confrontation of the patient's resistances and defenses and, contrary to Mann, he does not insist on a fixed limit to the treatment duration nor a commitment from the patient to maintain the focus of treatment. For Malan, the aim of treatment is the analysis of the impulse-anxiety-defense triad, what he calls the triangle of insight. The technique for accomplishing this aim remains relatively close to the nondirective stance of more classical treatment.

The triangle of insight involves the patient's awareness of conflict as this is encountered in relation to the therapist (T), in current relations with people (O), and in relation to significant people in the past (P). Working within the classical analytic model, the patient's conflicts are addressed via their defensive resistant characteristics and, when possible, the impulse is interpreted along with its accompanying anxiety. The focus of the treatment is maintained only when necessary. Thus, with oedipal patients, the focus is carried by the patients; with preoedipal cases, therapeutic activity to maintain focus consists of "selective interpretation, selective attention, and selective neglect" (Malan, 1976, p. 32). Thus Malan's approach to brief psychotherapy, apart from its limited aim and limited duration, serves as a model for brief psychoanalytic psychotherapy.

In Malan's model, the area within which the therapist chooses to work is dependent on the material the patient presents. This usually entails work on the patient's current life problems (O) and then shifts to the transference (T). The genetic material and the significance of early prototypic relationships (P) is usually interpreted last, after the other material has been clarified. Malan has found that interpretations of the parent-transference link is one of the most important elements in successful therapy using his approach.

Malan (1963) himself stated that one of the first important lessons he learned in his study of brief psychotherapy was that, despite efforts to deflect or bypass intense transferences, in many cases this was not possible. His reported cases, however, show no more serious difficulties with termination than do those cases reported by advocates of the nonregressive, manipulative treatment approach. Thus the assumption of most brief psychotherapists that the regressive pull of the classical psychoanalytic approach results in unmanageable transference paradigms is not, strictly speaking, correct. From our own perspective, although regression does pose a technical problem for a nondirective time limited treatment approach, other factors in the brief treatment situation probably serve to reduce its effects. Mann's interesting perspective on time and its use in time-limited brief psychotherapy provides one parameter of the treatment process which operates to limit the transference regression. The imposition of the time-limit seems to establish, for both patient and therapist, a finite context within which the transference paradigm is played out. Mann suggests that the time-limit establishes a beginning, middle, and end phase corresponding to the sequence of (1) a return to timelessness, (2) the reemergence of reality, and (3) termination. From the perspective of developments in the transference, such phases would correspond to the emergence of (1) positive transference, (2) disillusionment and the development of the negative transference resistance, and (3) termination, or the working through of the transference neurosis. We would suggest, then, that a time-limited psychoanalytic psychotherapy organized around a neutral therapeutic stance could serve as a model for studying the emergence, development, and working through of the transference neurosis.

Clearly, brief psychotherapies have many features that distinguish them from the more classical approach. It has been the purpose of this chapter to contrast these therapies to psychoanalysis from the perspective of therapeutic context and therapeutic stance vis-à-vis the transference. Our intent was not so much to criticize the brief psychotherapeutic approach as to juxtapose it to the classical stance to be described in subsequent chapters. In what follows, we will attempt to show that brief treatment can be modeled on the classical approach with respect to both its intent and therapeutic stance without leading to either catastrophic regression or interminable treatment. As such, it can be useful as a model for studying psychoanalytic process variables which have been exceedingly difficult to isolate because of the enormous amount of data generated by even the simplest analytic treatment. By way of bearing out this claim, we turn now to a case treated by a brief form of psychoanalytic psychotherapy.

4 Clinical Case Report: History and Overview of the Treatment Process

Having identified the major distinguishing features of the current brief dynamic psychotherapies in respect to the central issue of the analysis of the transference, we will now turn to the case study that forms the central focus of the present monograph. As an aid to grasping the complexities of this case and to articulating the specific transference paradigm that emerged, we will first present a brief history and summary of the main dynamic themes that developed over the course of the 14 treatment sessions. This first report summarizes the initial presentation of the patient and all the major trends as they evolved in the course of the treatment. This is followed in the next chapter by detailed summaries of each session. To better convey the mood of the sessions and provide concrete examples of how various subjects were broached and broadened by the patient or the therapist, and how the two of them interacted, verbatim excerpts are included in these detailed summaries. Each session is followed by our comments on the work of the session in which we spell out our clinical reading of the treatment course and development, and the intermingling of the various transference and extratransference themes. Our purpose there will be to highlight the specific technical issues that emerged in this brief treatment and to provide the reader with the data on which our inferences about transference will be based.

CLINICAL CASE REPORT

Mr. P. is one of a number of patients who was referred by the Cardiac Rehabilitation Clinic at Downstate Medical Center for psychotherapy.

The criteria for selection of these patients are that they have had a mycardial infarction no more than 3 months previously, are now ambulatory patients at the Rehabilitation Clinic, speak English adequately, are of at least average intelligence as indicated by a high school education, and are willing to enter a program of brief psychotherapy at no cost to themselves.

P. had no regular family physician; he was referred to the Rehabilitation Clinic by the physician who treated him at the hospital after his recent attack. His hospital stay was uneventful. The cardiologist at the clinic saw him once, and only for the purpose of arranging a stress test for him. His rehabilitation program consisted of an exercise program three times weekly. This program was supervised by one or another of the several physical education instructors who take turns in supervising patients. P. had, therefore, no continuing, meaningful relationship with any physician or therapist other than his psychotherapist during the period of psychotherapy itself or for some time before and after the period of therapy. Thus, as far as can be determined, there was no "splitting" of the transference.

P. attended 30 rehabilitation sessions and terminated of his own accord approximately 3 months after the completion of his psychotherapy program. His exercise program was uneventful. He showed a 20% improvement in his stress tolerance when he was tested 2 months after he terminated the program, an improvement that was considered "good" by the Rehabilitation Clinic.

P. is a 42-year-old Jewish man, an independent businessman with some college education, recently separated and living alone, except for his 7-year-old daughter who was with him half the week through a joint custody arrangement. Three months prior to the beginning of the treatment, the patient suffered a myocardial infarction. Through his physical rehabilitation program and in connection with the present research project, the patient was offered and accepted a free once-a-week psychotherapy treatment for 3 months, totaling 14 sessions. At the beginning of the therapy, P. stated how, prior to receiving this offer, he thought of looking for a therapist on his own because a "heart attack is a kind of heavy thing to deal with."

HISTORY

P. came from a struggling working-class family. His mother was described as a loving and wonderful person, and his father as an "emotionally ice-cold, dogmatic and narrow-minded" person who had little interest in the patient as he was growing up and trying to pursue artistic talents his mother encouraged. There was also a brother a couple of years older. As a teenager, the patient felt "sexual guilt," was a "klutz" when it came to sports, and felt ostracized by other boys for being inadequate. He majored in art but did not complete college; he started working and got married in his early 20s. The marriage dissolved after 2 years, with P. feeling abandoned and depressed, and entering intensive individual psychotherapy with an Adlerian trainee. He did not think much of his therapist in retrospect, but kept coming for a couple of years because the therapist "maintained" him. Eventually he became more socially active, his business picked up, and he became modestly successful and felt better. It was at that time, in his early 30s, that P. entered a rather expressive variety of group therapy in which he participated in marathon sessions and punched pillows ("immediately very helpful . . . in getting out the frustration, but long-term benefit open to doubt"). His father died a couple of years earlier, but P. "did not feel much grief" until a weekend marathon session when "somebody mentioned their father . . . and it just started gushing out of me, Daddy I love you, I love you." He was impotent for "6 or 10 months" as he "worked on" his father.

It was at this time that he met a woman with whom he "had great sex" and after some hesitation and pressure from her, he suddenly married her. After an ideal honeymoon trip and "the best wedding that anybody ever went to," they had a "pretty good first 3 years." During this period, they had a daughter, but business was not very successful. They began to drift apart, and one day, in his late 30s, he "became completely psychosomatic . . . couldn't move [his] legs" and started seeing Dr. S., a neighborhood psychiatrist. There followed 2 years of individual therapy of a very eclectic and pragmatic sort about which P. felt very positive. About a year after this therapy ended, P. discovered that his wife was having an affair. When she would not stop it, he left her. Now, a year later, they still live in the same neighborhood and their 7-year-old daughter spends half a week with each of them. He somehow put off finalizing their separation, partly because of the heart attack he suffered 3 months earlier.

TREATMENT COURSE

From the first minutes of the initial session, the patient was very talkative and open. However, he did not dwell at all on the problem of his medical condition. Despite his initial feeling that his heart attack was the occasion for the therapy, he promptly concentrated on his long-term problems and preoccupations. He was most eloquent when it came to criticizing his wife, her defects, and all the "dirty crap" to which she subjected him. In session 1, he managed to disclose a great deal about himself, including the fact that he "had homosexual experiences." Yet he was very vague and evasive when the therapist attempted to clarify moot points. It was as if he was inviting the therapist to extricate the "truth" by aggressive persistent questioning, an invitation the therapist did not accept. Some of P.'s evasiveness had to do with the nihilism and resignation which he clearly expresses in this session: "There are problems in life which I've, I've sort of given up the hope of changing myself radically. I don't think that the change that I would like is possible." In light of this attitude, it was not surprising that he evaded and sidestepped a question which repeatedly was raised by the therapist in the first three sessions, i.e., what would he like to change about himself? That he "never made enough money" and was a "passive, not aggressive type" was the most explicit he could be about himself. Indirectly, however, P. was much more revealing. In session 2, he implicitly linked his feelings of inadequacy as a person, and especially as a male, with the love and approval that his father withheld from him. Yet, he passed up an opportunity to talk more about these issues and perhaps explicitly connect them, and instead went on to describe his various adventures with women in general and especially his wife. Thus he repeats with the therapist what it will subsequently become clear he has been doing throughout his life, i.e., he assuages his painful feelings of inadequacy by "proving" himself manly in exploits with women. Thus, he describes how, in his therapy 11 years earlier, he dealt with "working" on his father and the related impotence problem by getting involved with his wife-to-be with a gargantuan sexual appetite and grand style.

In session 3, the patient talked of how he not only would like, but how much he needs somebody to take him by the hand, to tell him what he should and should not do, and how he cannot be trusted to look after his own best interests. He talked again of feeling inferior to other men, and after much homosexual-passive imagery, he once more openly mentioned his homosexuality. He reported feeling "high" after the previous session because he could get the load off his chest by telling the therapist about his homosexuality, but in the very act of talking about this "high" positive feeling, he breaks into a cold sweat and has the thought that his father would kill him if he knew about it. It is a fair possibility that at this moment P. experienced a homosexual impulse, or a fear of such an impulse, toward the therapist. The wish, expressed earlier in this session, that "somebody" (i.e., the therapist) lead and regulate him, supports this possibility.

In session 4 the patient continued to weave a matrix in which he connected themes of homosexuality and death (e.g., a pain in his anus in the middle of the previous night which makes him suspect a colonic cancer); incestuous feelings and aloneness (e.g., he was closer to his mother than father and now he fears he and his daughter are "too close"); being helped and being seduced (e.g., he does not like seeing a proctologist because it reminds him of how his pediatrician reportedly made passes at his mother). He also talked of his inability to change himself and fondly remembered Dr. X. with whom he felt more like a friend than a patient who came because of his neurosis. He likened the present therapist's "relaxed demeanor" to that of Dr. X, thereby linking the themes of this session to the developing transference with his current therapist.

In session 5, he complained of "paying for people to do nothing" and how it drives him crazy when somebody speaks slowly, or is not "moving fast enough", in the context of how he feels he did "only one-fourth of the things [he] wanted to do in life." He said he had a "bad, nauseous" feeling when talking of his fear of not performing up to his parent's standards. He came 20 minutes late to session 6, and blamed it on "dealing with somebody who's moving very slowly." He dwelt briefly on his fears of not being aggressive and masculine enough, and confided that he has carried on a love affair with his teenage sister-in-law for years. He talked in some detail—in a by now familiar, grandiose manner—about the great times they had sexually ("had sex three times a day for 5 weeks") but concluded the session with a diatribe against promiscuous wives. He arrived early for the seventh session and began with vague complaints similar to the previous two sessions: he got depressed after the last session, and now misidentifies the subject matter of this session as being about his father. He described how he was pushing his voice to talk during the past week, and was saying things he himself did not quite understand to a single man who made him uptight by suggesting they go to the theater and "do something together." When the therapist gently attempted to explore the transference basis and implications of this panicky feeling by asking P. how he has felt talking with him over this period, the patient reaffirmed that he feels comfortable with the therapist and his "relaxed demeanor."

The lateness in the previous session, the complaints about people "not moving fast enough" in the last few sessions, references to the pleasurable closeness with Dr. X., and this latest fear of closeness with a man have important transference implications. Absent are his pronouncements that he expects no change—but his eagerness, even impatience, is expressed through latenesses and irritation rather than by doing therapeutic work. He clearly wants and expects "something" from the therapist, but is so far unable to express it appropriately. He does, however, have a predominantly positive transference which, in session 7, leads to expressions of optimism about therapy: "How do I get cured? I want to stop this crap and start living." It is also important to note that he has not, up to this point, halfway through the treatment, in any way commented on the two main treatment parameters—that it is short-term, time-limited and that it is free. This is despite the fact that all his previous therapy experiences were exactly the opposite—long-term and for a fee. Later in this session, possibly protected and encouraged by his positive transference feelings, he brought up and analyzed an old castration fantasy which he, for the first time, related to his father, mother, and himself. In session 8, he complained of "not having slept in three nights," and of a general deterioration in his functioning. Several times, now, after finishing the preceding session on an upbeat note, he starts the next one in a resistant, even oppositional manner. This change is most evident at this juncture (session 7 to 8), and has reached a point where he is, for the moment, unable, to continue with the therapeutic work: he was unable, first to remember, and then, when reminded, to explore further the oedipal material from the previous session. It is at this timely juncture that the therapist inquires about the here-and-now transference issues, and this finally enables the patient to express anger at the therapist for the shortness of the treatment, saying, "it is too late now" for him to "push down the stuff" that had been coming up. He even hinted that the therapist may have wanted to lure him into a long-term and financially burdensome treatment by offering free sessions at first. He felt like smashing "something" (i.e., the therapist). However, in response to repeated interpretations, the patient not only moves away from this paranoid-accusatory tone to one of expressing his concerns more maturely, but he is also able to link these current feelings with his response to his father's death and, more generally, to his frustrations in trying to relate to his father since childhood. In session 9, the patient begins rather casually, but within a couple of minutes, he cries and professes to be falling to pieces. He is less aggressive toward the therapist, but clearly more depressed and lost. He now more intensely pleads with the therapist not to leave him, both directly ("I will have to continue therapy. . . . Is it possible for you to take me on as a private patient?") and indirectly ("I'm falling apart because of this here." "I feel like saying to you, 'I want to commit suicide.'") However, by the end of this session, he expresses himself in a more mature, appropriate way, reflecting earlier therapeutic work that has addressed this issue. As these attempts were interpreted, the patient responded by airing further childhood fears relating to his oedipal situation and later problems with exhibitionism in puberty and adulthood, although he was not yet capable of integrating these issues with transference interpretations. He also retells a story with which he opened the session; it concerns a drinking binge the night before with a bisexual male friend. Now, however, he tells the story in such a way that its symbolically explicit homosexual character becomes obvious, although P. does not explicitly acknowledge it. In an almost ingenious combination of acting-out and acting-in, he gets into "a big screaming cursing fight" with his most important, father-like client on the morning of session 10, and cannot make it to the session on time. For a variety of reasons, the therapist agrees to "reschedule" the session for the next day. In the session, possibly heartened by this "gift," the patient appears much more stable than in sessions 8 and 9. He feels depressed, empty, insecure, but stops his self-destructive attempts to induce the therapist to continue seeing him beyond the 14 sessions. But he is still open about his strong feelings regarding the end of the therapy: he wants to throw the chair through the window, feels like throwing up, and so on, even as he manages to continue with the therapeutic work.

He is slightly late to session 11, but seems in good control of himself; he lets the therapist know that social and business matters have priority over the therapy. He now denies being upset about the pending termination. However, he continues to do productive work, piecing together the circumstances in which, when he was 3 to 5 years old, his brother's appendix was taken out, the family went bankrupt, and his father left them for almost a year before they caught up with him.

In session 12, he continued complaining of poor functioning, but seemed much less upset. He talked again about his present situation and expressed an opinion that he has "built a block, not wanting to dig further, not wanting to start anything because this [therapy] is coming to an end." Together with anger at his wife, he also expressed a disappointed realization that he still feels a great deal of hurt that they broke up. He talked of feeling "not valid enough" to pursue other women sexually in a more assertive way, even though he wished to do so.

Throughout this session, the patient seems to oscillate between two poles: on one, he starts with omnipotent phallic impulses and, in the wake of their failure, paranoid, sadomasochistic impulses take over; on the other, a depressed and deflated, yet calmer and more functional image of himself emerges. Although he does not seem to understand these circular dynamics, he no longer appears in danger of manically riding his impulses until the bitter end. Rather, he seems to have become better able to bear a "depressive" stance in which he relinquishes certain fantasies and impulses for the sake of a reasonably functional existence.

This uneasy equilibrium remains the hallmark of the last two sessions (13 and 14). He reported more instances of aggression-laden sexual impulses toward women he met or just passed on the street. Ambivalence abounded: together with thoughts of how good it would feel to beat up his wife, he spontaneously admitted to longing for her affection. He spoke both of wanting a stable relationship with one woman, and of aggressively approaching and having sex with a great many women. He denied any current homosexual wishes, but said, "it comes back when I'm not involved with women." Yet, the idea of eliminating it completely would have made him feel he "dropped a whole area of [his] life." He talked of worries of growing old alone, of his child growing up and leaving him. When this was interpreted in terms of the therapy ending, he agreed, but professed no need for further therapy. He struggled to maintain the posture of an independent mature adult ("I just gotta shit or get off the pot and nobody can do that for me"), and, in line with this posture, occasional anger not withstanding, expressed his warm feelings and appreciation for the therapist and for the progress made in the therapy ("I'm a lot calmer than I was . . . I don't think I'm as high-strung as when I came here"). He was more tolerant and aware of his many ambivalences, and allowed himself to experience himself as a more vulnerable and less perfect individual. He seemed to accept this self-assessment with a mixture of resignation and sadness as well as relief and even realistic optimism; these feelings contrasted with the rage of earlier sessions. But his new equilibrium remained precarious, and P. still had to cope with his fears via an array of poorly understood impulses that encompassed quasi-omnipotent, homosexual-passive and heterosexual-aggressive maneuvers. His continuing reliance on these maneuvers gained expression in an exchange that occurred 5 to 7 minutes before the end of the last session:

> . . . Like right now I feel like I'm getting senile. I feel like my brain is going to sleep. I need an electric shock therapy or something, some electric, electric shock up my ass, that's what I need . . . drained of all my intellectual energy, psychic energy. I need something really exciting.

When asked, "What do you consider exciting?" he replied: "Oh, I would love to produce a play or climb a mountain or do a colossal piece of art work or have a, you know, 48-hour sexual marathon with my sister-in-law."

SUMMARY

P. developed a strong positive transference toward the therapist. With this transference acting as an "umbrella" and a catalyst, he was able to face his fears of having been castrated and abandoned, forever, doomed to look to older men as a source of strength and to reassure himself of his masculine adequacy via sexually aggressive interactions with women who, so he feared, would leave him once they discovered he was no stronger than them. As soon as these conflicts became activated, the initial positive transference, as such, could no longer be maintained. Moreover, the parameters of the treatment exerted influence in the same direction: after the initial seductive effect of the free sessions came the withdrawing, abandoning quality of the time-limited, short-term treatment. P. reacted to this threat of "parental" abandonment with regression to passive-homosexual, aggressive-heterosexual, and even self-destructive tendencies. Under the influence of the therapist's neutrality and consistently active interpretation of transference and acting-out behavior, however, the patient, possibly for the first time in his life, continued to explore—and to question the adaptive value of—certain of his defensive strategies. The new equilibrium that began to emerge was that of a sadder, less inflated, but freer and less burdened man. The final sessions, be it noted, were insufficient to provide a full working-through experience. Furthermore, under the influence of the termination, the patient felt an even greater need to rely on his most proven defenses. Thus, despite some new alignments in his psyche, the more primitive elements remained prominent to the end, along with fragile new elements of a more adaptive nature.

5

Clinical Case Report: Session-by-Session Analysis

In the previous chapter, we presented an overview of the dynamics and course of the 14-session treatment that our patient underwent. Having acquainted the reader with the general outlines of the treatment course and the main lines along which interpretive efforts were directed, we can now proceed with a detailed description of each of the treatment sessions, and comments about the way each of the main issues were dealt with in these sessions.

Our focus in this chapter is on tracing the gradual development of the transference: from initial positive transference, with strong passive homosexual strivings repeated in the relation to the therapist; to subsequent negative transference feelings, with strong anger and intense castration feelings repeated in relation to the therapist; to a final phase of partial working through of these feelings and the emergence and partial working through of feelings of loss and separation resulting from the termination of the short-term treatment. Although the brevity of the treatment course resulted in a telescoping of the transference issues, it is our belief that the essential lines of an analytic process were established and maintained throughout. An initial positive transference developed and was rapidly transformed into an organized negative transference as the patient's dependency on the analyst turned into hostile feelings as a result of the patient's experience of castration at the hands of the cold rejecting and abandoning father. The partial working through of these feelings set the stage for the termination phase of the treatment and the partial working through of separation issues.

In this chapter, we will present a relatively complete summary of each session, followed by our comments about the process occurring in the session. This format will enable the reader to follow our thinking about the ongoing process and to evaluate critically the way the main lines of transference analysis were conducted in this treatment. We believe that such a format is necessary for systematic research on process variables

SESSION 1

After receiving P.'s permission to tape the session, the therapist asks if he had any trouble finding "this place?" "None," P. says, but he wishes this hospital was located some place else, explaining that the taxi costs him about $7 each way. This slight exaggeration prompts the therapist to ask how he felt about coming to see him today.

> Uh, I was very glad when Dr. S. suggested it. . . . Half the effect of the heart attack is in the head, as you are probably well aware, and, uh, I was thinking of calling the heart association to see if there were any programs for counseling and therapy after a heart attack, um, 'cause it's a kind of heavy thing to deal with. . . . I'm young, only 42, and I have a 7-year-old daughter I have half the time; my wife and I just split up and I was in a state of depression before I had the heart attack. . . . Afterwards, I really found it devastating, um, scared . . . you know, you feel vulnerable. . . .

In response to a question of how long he's been depressed, P. says he saw a couple of different doctors over the past 20 years. The last one was "a local doctor, a wonderful psychiatrist" and he saw him for about 3 years until 2 years ago. "And then my wife and I split; a very, very bad separation. I found her in bed with a neighbor, and she's a real bitch. . . . I'm the kind of guy that takes things like that very, very hard." He goes on to describe how his wife went to this neighbor's house across the street and how he actually saw her in bed with him through the window. "Well, I literally started trembling all over, which I do when I get very nervous, and I went and broke his front door down. It was right out of a cheap novel." He made his wife promise she would not see that man, but she continued seeing him ("I couldn't stand him, he was an out-of-work longshoreman and the guy never bathed, he was really a disgusting, vile character"). He decided, "that's it, I'm moving out and within 30 days, I was out." He goes on to describe how, on a recent occasion, his wife wanted to keep from him some reimbursement money which was his, and he is about to bring up more examples when the therapist interrupts to ask what brought him to the first psychiatrist he saw? The answer was depression following his first marriage, which ended in a divorce in his early 20s: "I tend to be a loner. I don't want to be that way, but that's the way I am, and after I got divorced the first time, I really withdraw when things like that happen. I tried to become an alcoholic and failed at that, uh, I started drinking a lot and getting sick, not drunk but sick." A friend of his referred him to the Adler Clinic. "[I] was interviewed by Alexandra Adler, which was very interesting, and then was referred to a psychologist who was not very good. Went to him for a couple of years and then dropped out and then went . . . [to a group which] was like primal therapy, it wasn't but it was very intense, uh, emotional outpouring kind of thing. You could beat up pillows and scream and so on, which I went to for several years and found . . . immediately helpful. Long range was open to question, but short range very, very helpful to get out the tension, uh, and so on, uh, and then [I] ended up with Dr. X., a really fine man." P describes him as a "mensch." "[He was] a marvelous person to talk to. It wasn't a doctor-patient relationship. It was like talking to a very, very close warm friend. It was really marvelous. Anyway, he moved out. . . ." The patient reiterates Dr. X's moving was not the reason he stopped coming, but that they "both felt it was necessary." He added: "My feeling is that there are problems in life which, uh, I've, I've sort of given up the hope of really changing myself radically. Uh, I don't think that, that the change that I would like, that would be ideal, is possible." When the therapist asks what would he like to change, P. talks about his one-man business, the tensions and pressures associated with it, and relates a recent business disappointment. "I'm not scheduled for success." The therapist asks about his present relationship with his wife. They "talk occasionally," but "it's not a good relationship. I hate her." They are still not legally separated. "Uh, she's been procrastinating, I was procrastinating in the beginning, then she was putting it off, then after the heart attack, my doctor said not to start with it right away cause I was very strung out" but he will "start the process soon" even though he "hates getting into it." The patient starts complaining his wife is not giving him proceeds from a small house they own. The therapist asks about the first therapist P. saw. The patient repeats that he does not think much of him in retrospect, and answers a question about why then did he stay with him that long. "I don't think I knew any better." However, he also feels the first therapist helped because he "maintained" and "consoled" him. The therapist then asks P. to tell him about his early life. He is "a native of New Jersey, grew up in uh, lower middle-class Jewish family, uh, one brother, four years older . . . had a relatively normal childhood, uh, with, I've always had problems. . . ." (Therapist:

Can you recall any right now?) "Uhm, a lot of sexual problems when I was a kid, in where I fit, what role . . . uh . . . I belonged in, what niche I belonged in." (You mean whether you were a boy or a girl?) "Well, I've had some homosexual experiences . . . do not in any way consider myself a homosexual. I think it's more . . . a . . . reaching out for contact with other people and that's the easiest way to do it, which, I think, is why a lot of homosexuals do it . . . uh . . . I was always kind of a loner, I always felt a lot of pain and stress. I was never really very happy, you know, things have never, never gone nice and easy."

The therapist then asks about his parents. P. describes his father as "emotionally ice-cold." He died over a decade ago in his early 60s. His mother is, however, "still living and . . . a marvelous, very nice person . . . we have a very nice adult relationship now, which I'm very glad about." However, he worries about her getting older and feels demeaned that he still owes her some money and repays it irregularly even though she lives only on social security. Then he talks about his older brother; they are "quite different" and were even more so when the patient was younger. However, when he had the heart attack, his brother "stepped right in and did what a good brother is supposed to do. Really took care of things. Picked me up from the hospital, brought me to his house, you know." When they were growing up, though, they fought all the time. "He gave me claustrophobia . . . when I first got my sleeping bag . . . as a boy scout . . . he zipped me up and sat on me and wouldn't let me out." His brother's "marvelous kids" remind him of how he misses "family warmth and love. . . . We used to make the seder the last few years, and, uh, I'm not a religious person but . . . my biggest disappointment in separating is that I no longer make a seder." Both his and his wife's family "whom I got along with very well" would come.

The therapist asks what he thinks led to the breakup, the disruption between him and his wife? "We were married 10 years, I think the last 7, since [the venture they worked on jointly] went [down], since my daughter was born. They both happened at the same time." They do not fulfill one another's expectations. She is "one of the world's worst slobs . . . her house was always filthy, clothes all over the place, nothing taken care of. She was a telephone addict," and so on. When the therapist asks for a clarification as to whether he is talking about his present or his first wife, the patient remarks he "can hardly remember" his first wife. "It was a long, long time ago. We were only married for 2 years and 4 months and 6 days. We were both kids. The first, the first marriage is really insignificant." (Why did that break up?) "Uh . . . I also married the wrong woman. I, I like to sit at home and listen to music and look at art and discuss philosophy. My first wife was a social butterfly . . . she was really a different type. I was 24 and she was 19, and I think that's really too young to get married. I think that's ridiculous."

The therapist asks how he thinks he is responsible for the difficulties in the marriage? P. replies it is because he "never made enough money, which can lead to a lot of other problems," and because he "tends to be somewhat passive, not aggressive type." He recalls how his wife once offered to support him so he could close his business in order to sculpt and paint. But "then she'll turn around and say you never made enough money, so she's all mixed up." He goes on to describe another affair she had "with another guy I know." She "kept bringing him home." They worked together and he would drive her home and "the whole time she was having an affair with him." Eventually she told him about it. "I remember we were in a restaurant, my legs started shaking, I couldn't stand up [laughter] . . . Eventually I forgave her, it passed. I think I always, of course, harbored feelings about it, uh, he was, as it happens, I'm not a very prejudiced person, but he was Black. Which has its effect, I mean, it has its purpose [long pause]. So she did me a lot of dirty crap. I'm no angel either." (Therapist: What do you mean by that? That you had affairs, too?) "Uh, not very much, but after I was married several years, I started playing around a little bit."

The therapist now asks what he thinks was "the main contributing factor" to his getting a heart attack, what was on his mind just before the attack? P. prefaces his answer by saying he is "strictly an 'A-type' person," that he was always very tense, running around. "I was so hyper that it was ridiculous." It happened on a "bitter cold night in February." He visited a friend who also "just went through a divorce and his wife too went crazy and had a very terrible separation, so we commiserated. We were talking about separation, which we do when we get together, about how bitchy our wives are and how lousy they treated us and we wished they'd get hit by trucks, you know, mostly, kind of." Then as he started walking home and "these terrible pains" started, he couldn't explain to his daughter what was going on. "I was sure I was going to drop dead in the street, and my daughter would be standing there." The pains passed as he reached home and lay down, but they started again in the morning, "so I ended up in the hospital." The therapist then says they do not "have much more time left today" and that "this is a relatively brief program of psychotherapy lasting about oh, roughly 3 months, once a week." He gives the patient an inventory form to fill out and schedules the patient to take psychological tests with another doctor. The patient asks:

Pt.:   How long are these sessions?
Th.:   Forty-five minutes with me. Do you have any questions that you want to ask of me?
Pt.:   Uh, well, none that one of the doctors will answer is how long am I gonna live? That's, well, nobody can tell me that.

The therapist declines to discuss his medical condition and they part mentioning, once again, the time for the psychological testing.

Comment

After some initial complaints about the location of the hospital and exaggerating the car service charge he paid, P. hastens to point out his genuine motivation for the therapy. Within minutes, he is revealing intimate details of his life, with an ease that is remarkable considering that this is his first session. However, he is most eloquent and talkative when it comes to talking about his wife, her defects and all the "dirty crap" she did to him. In addition to being a resistance to talking about himself, and reflecting the extent to which projective mechanisms are operative in P., this probably also represents his attempt to establish with the therapist a sort of rapport similar to the one he experienced with his previous therapist, and perhaps even like the one with his commiserating friend with whom he exchanged violent stories and fantasies about their wives. The therapist, at first probably quite intuitively, reacts to these excessive discussions about P.'s wife by cutting him off and opening other subjects for discussion. The therapist is, of course, also motivated by getting, as soon as possible, a comprehensive overview of P.'s current conflicts, developmental issues, and so on. P. makes this both easy and difficult: difficult, by mentioning clearly central issues, only to gloss over them. (He "had some homosexual experiences" but does not "in any way consider himself a homosexual"; it's just "a reaching out for contact with other people"; or he talks in detail of his wife's two affairs, but dismisses his own: ". . . after I was married several years, I started playing around a little bit.") But he makes it easy, too, by a peculiar ability of his unconscious to upstage his denials. (His first marriage is "really insignificant" and he "can hardly remember" his first wife, yet mentions the duration of that marriage to the very last day.) This creates a somewhat bizarre feel to the session, in that the patient frustrates the therapist's attempts to get a clearer picture of some issues, only to reveal, unexpectedly, some other crucial information. This tendency may even be somewhat unconscious and is probably a part of the patient's style and self-image as a clown. Just as he is "the kind of guy" who "tried to become an alcoholic and failed; [got] sick, not drunk but sick"; who comments on his rage at his wife's infidelity with "it was right out of a cheap novel"; whose boy scout sleeping bag ends up giving him claustrophobia rather than pride; so, too, it may be part of his "style" to expose his "weaknesses" even as he tries to present himself as a tough, resolute character. His unconscious races to bring up problems which he then minimizes.

This evasiveness must stem, at least partly, from an attitude he openly expresses: why bring up painful issues if nothing can be done about them, or, in his words, ". . . there are problems in life which I've, I've sort of given up the hope of really changing myself radically. I don't think that . . . the change that I would like, that would be ideal, is possible." This statement comes in the midst of P.'s praise for his previous therapist with whom he felt not just "accepted" with all his problems, but from whom he apparently also got the message that he need not (or should not, or cannot) do anything major about these problems. In addition to enhancing a positive feeling of being accepted and being OK (and therefore feeling it was "marvelous" to talk with Dr. X.), this relationship with Dr. X reinforced his passive, depressive tendencies and feelings that he could not change himself or his predicaments. Therefore, not surprisingly, P. evades a straight or serious answer to the question of what things he would like to change about himself. He small-talks about pressures and failures in his business, expressing the sentiment that he is not "scheduled" for success. This choice of a word, usually associated closely with therapy sessions, further reflects P.'s underlying assumptions about therapy and how much he can and cannot expect of it.

The most explicit statement of his problems that the patient manages is that he "never made enough money" and is "passive, not aggressive type." This is related to feelings of vulnerability. He was too suspicious to accept his wife's offer of support should he have pursued an artistic career. He seems to feel unable to accomplish things on his own, yet is afraid of depending on others. He talks disparagingly of his wife, but admits his own reluctance to finalize their breakup, which he found to be "really . . . devastating." Similarly, he puts down his first therapist, yet explains away his staying in therapy with him for years as being due to the fact that the therapist "maintained" him.

Although the therapist has to ask a number of questions to clarify what P. is really saying, thereby also letting him know that he is aware of the apparent inconsistencies in his productions, he does not systematically or exhaustively pursue them. There are a number of reasons for this. First, in this initial session, the therapist has a great deal to learn about the patient's style, to assess how much of it is conscious or unconscious, and so on; second is the fact that excessive direction from the therapist at this point would distort the way the patient chooses to present himself. Thus the therapist's restraint allows the patient, at least initially, to choose the depth to which he will go in speaking of his problems. By asking for occasional clarifications, the therapist lets the patient know he is aware of a conflictual theme and encourages him to speak in greater detail about it, but he does not pursue such themes fully in the initial sessions. This ensures that the therapist will have a good idea of the patient's defenses and of what his economic realities are, that is, how far the patient feels capable of pursuing conflicts without running away from them or even decompensating. This kind of judgment is crucial to make in short-term therapy because the therapist, throughout the treatment, has to navigate between pushing the patient to confront his problems more deeply or extensively than heretofore, and yet not pushing him past a point beyond which the patient has little chance of resolving these problems by the end of treatment. As we have previously indicated, a number of short-term therapy approaches attempt to solve, or rather preempt this problem by selecting a single focus (e.g., issues of dependency and separation, or certain oedipal conflicts). Although such selection does simplify treatment, it does so at the expense of limiting the therapist to an approach that may not be as powerfully related to the patient's core conflicts as it might otherwise be.[1] In our approach, the therapist does not have a preference for dealing with one kind of conflict rather than another, but he attempts to achieve the maximum that the patient's ego strength and current transference dynamics will allow, using whatever constellations are prominently present in the general and transference material.

The therapist's relative passivity in this session also has to do with this particular patient. There is an almost teasing quality in P.'s half-revelations about himself. While he works hard on presenting himself as a motivated and interesting patient, he often does not reveal even as much as he is consciously aware of, attempting instead to induce the therapist to extricate the information from him by aggressive questioning. This fashion of relating would have surely influenced the subsequent transference developments in the direction of passive–

---

[1]The major liability of such an "active" stance to the patient's conflicts is the effect of this activity in the transference. As a form of manipulation of the transference, it is unlikely that it will be subsequently addressed interpretively. This issue will be taken up in Chapter 7, where we discuss the question of how one establishes a focus in this form of psychoanalytic brief psychotherapy.

aggressive, sado-masochistic conflicts so central to this patient, but which would be so much more difficult to analyze or control if they were acted on in the treatment.

Another most remarkable feature of this session is that the patient does not in any way mention the two main parameters of the therapy he is initiating: that it is short-term, time-limited, and that it is free. His opening exaggeration of the carefare he paid should probably be understood as a defensive attempt to state that he is, after all, paying for sessions, even if indirectly. Still, this omission is all the more remarkable coming from someone who had a number of previous therapies that were long-term and open-ended and for which he did pay a fee. In line with the overall approach, the therapist does not bring up these issues at this point.[2]

SESSION 2

P. starts by commenting on how "very interesting" he found the questionnaire that the therapist gave him. However, "after filling that thing out and arriving at a personality profile, or whatever, it looked terrible. . . . the questionnaire asked a lot of questions that I don't like asking myself, uh, because it all represents failure in a lot of, lot of areas, and it was kind of, a little bit depressing . . . I don't like a lot of things about my life. . . ." The therapist asks about things that P. would like to make changes in, but P. avoids the question and only indirectly responds by relating an episode over the weekend that made him feel apologetic and uneasy for no good reason. "I always, I don't feel, uh, valid or entitled." Asked why he feels that way, P. recalls a teenage memory of his mother "showing off" with him, holding out a painting of his for a neighbor to see, which he found "so embarrassing." When he got to college, he "froze up" when he "had to sit down and create." As he says all this, he adds "I know I'm rambling" and concludes that even though he does his work fairly well and is confident, "as a human being and relating to other people, I get very uptight."

The therapist now asks about P.'s reactions to the psychological testing he took the other day. "Uh, . . . I'll tell you, the fellow that was giving it was very uptight." He goes on to say that drawing human figures made *him* feel "very uptight." Also, he became "competitive" on "the part that was measuring my awareness of general knowledge

---

[2] An additional parameter of this treatment that also does not draw any reaction from the patient is that the treatment sessions are audio-recorded.

or something" because, although "not dumb," he is very self-conscious about not having completed his formal college education. This reminds him of how he is not at all a sports fan, unlike "most men that live in our culture." He recalls never being athletic; when "forced into playing softball, invariably I used to run into a wall . . . real clumsy klutz." There "were a bunch of tough guys" in his school who would chorus him with "Here comes the faggot." Toward the end of elementary school, he "was with a very small group of the intellectual elite." He was a "goody, goody-good kid" and his mother was very active in the P.T.A. and would have P. bring his teachers cookies for Christmas, which he hated. He never confronted his mother about that, though.

The therapist now asks how P. felt about their session last week. "Uh, well, it feels kinda good to be talking to somebody again, because, as I said, I haven't been in therapy for a long time and also felt there should be therapy after a heart attack." He's been "running [around] a lot, so [he] didn't really make an evaluation." Still he "do[es] feel relief talking." The therapist asks whether one of the reasons P. was so pleased with his last psychiatrist, Dr. X., was that "in a way he kind of made up for the father that you didn't have or would have liked to have had." P. enthusiastically affirms this. "Everybody said of Dr. X. he was everybody's father or grandfather." P. has "a great deal of affection for older men." He recalls how he had beautifully hit it off with his wife's grandfather who died last year. "He gave me some of his tools . . . that he had been using for 60 years . . . very symbolic." This grandfather was, by trade, similar to P.'s own father, and there were "a lot of parallels." He relates how he had a chance to do this man a favor before he died and how good it made him feel. He likes doing things for older people and thinks many families neglect them and the whole society "stinks when it comes to its older people."

Th.: How did you get along with your own father?
Pt.: We had a kind of formal relationship. My father was unable to show any affection. When he was very ill one time in the hospital, maybe a year or two before he died, and I had to give him a shave *and it was terrible* because I had never touched my father, and I really felt like I was getting so personal with him, giving him a shave that it, it really made me *uptight.* Uh . . . I saw him the day before he died, two days before he died, he died during Passover and we shook hands which we very seldom do. We never kissed, that was, you know, out of the question. Uh, never had any physical contact.

P. goes on to relate how his father "didn't break down and didn't let it out" when he heard of his mother's death. "The only emotion he showed was that his hands started trembling a little bit and then he went back to finishing" what he was doing. He recalls, in response to a question, how his father never took him places. "The last thing that I can remember is going to the aquarium or to a zoo, but that was like 5 years old." Father was closer to his brother, who chose a vocation more similar to his. P., however, was "an artist ever since [he] was a little kid," and was closer to mother. He felt misunderstood by his father. "It was difficult to talk to him a lot of times as I started getting older, I started developing mentally. There was not too much common ground. Uh, he once picked up a painting out of a book he wanted me to copy. I wasn't interested in copying a painting. I was into my own thing. He didn't understand that. And he was, he had a moral code that nobody could live up to." Sexuality was "something terrible." The patient felt very embarrassed about "masturbating maybe three to four hundred times a day, always in the bathroom in secret. . . ."

Th.:   How did you feel when you began to have dates and so on?
Pt.:   One of the complaints that women have had toward me and still have, I mean I'm just a little older. I would go out with a woman and I would wine and dine her and not expect a kiss goodnight until the third date. Things haven't been that way for a long time. I mean, now you go out and you say hello and you jump into bed and you screw. I have a hard time getting used to that.

He has "been celibate" since he split with his wife (partly) because he cannot afford to treat dates in a lavish style. "It's cabs, it's dinners, the theater afterward, that's my style." Women themselves tell him he is not aggressive enough. Yet, he feels he has been "a little more demanding now" and relates how he stopped seeing, after a few times, a woman from his neighborhood because "she had a sexual hangup and . . . wouldn't perform fellatio and wouldn't have intercourse, so I couldn't go out with her." He enjoys her company and she is very nice, but he "can't deal with a woman who will go to bed and not have intercourse; it's just insane." The therapist asks how sex was with his wife? "The first couple of years it was terrific." Still, he recalls how, on their second date, they:

> went to my loft, danced to some music. When we were at the loft, I noticed Joan throw a cigarette butt into the garbage. And I thought, gee that's not a smart thing to do. Then we went to her place. She lived a few blocks from me. Then we jumped into bed and we screwed mightily. Now I had been in therapy. I had been working on my father for the first time ever he had come up or, and I suddenly became impotent. I'd been impotent for 6 months or 10 months, something like that. And Joan was the first woman I was able to really have a good time and have no problems, no sexual prob-

lems. We really went at it. Came home in the morning, my loft had burned down and everything I owned had burned down. I had a duplex loft, one of the most beautiful lofts in Manhattan.

He ended up in a hospital because of a back injury sustained as he was trying to keep his apartment from getting inundated by rainfall the next day. He feels in that instance that his wife had acted very insensitively toward his loss. "Thinking about it 10 years after the fact, she's a fucking bitch." However, a few weeks later, they met again; he moved in with her and they "spent the first 2 weeks screwing. . . . Just absolutely fantastic. . . . We enjoyed each other intellectually also." Later they drifted apart because they had "a very different way of looking at aesthetic experience; she was too analytic . . . too textbook trained." Still, "the first 3 years were pretty good." At her nudging, one day he finally proposed; they took a honeymoon trip to Mexico, and on their return, they had "the best wedding that anybody ever went to."

Comment

P. starts this session with depressing failure(s) in a lot of areas." He doesn't like "a lot of things about [his] life." But, as in the previous session, he evades talking specifically about them and summarily says that ". . . as a human being and relating to other people [he] get[s] very uptight." The therapist lets him do that and, possibly trying to get to the same issue through its transference manifestations and derivatives, asks about how P. experienced the psychological testing session. P. alternately labels both the tester and himself as "very uptight," and, as the continuing use of this adjective heralds, proceeds to talk about the sources of his insecurities, from the superficial (incomplete education, not being a sporting type) to the deeper ones (he was "a real clumsy klutz" and others called him a "faggot"). When the therapist asks about his feelings about their session the previous week, P. responds cautiously, that is, he "didn't really have time to make an evaluation." Further question about the similarities between P.'s previous therapist, Dr. X., and P.'s father, bring up memories of his father never showing him any affection, not appreciating him and setting impossible moral goals for him.

Thus the patient implicitly links his feelings of inadequacy as a person, and especially as a male, with the love and approval that his father withheld from him. Yet he passes up an opportunity to talk more about these issues and maybe explicitly connect them, and instead goes on to describe his various adventures with women in general and especially with his wife. Thus he does in the session what he apparently has been doing during the course of his life generally: he attempts to assuage his painful feelings of inadequacy by "proving" himself in exploits with women. He describes how, 11 years earlier, he dealt with "working" on his father in therapy and his related impotence by getting involved with his wife-to-be with a gargantuan sexual appetite and in a grand style.

The therapist does not get far when he asks directly about the things P. does not like about his life. However, when he probes for transference derivatives (by asking about P.'s experience of the psychological testing session), the patient quite freely rambles in much more detail about his problems. When the therapist now asks more directly about transferential material (i.e., about P.'s feelings about their first session), the patient is again vague and cautious. The therapist switches once more to a less charged topic by asking about parallels between P.'s last therapist and his father, and P. is more open and informative. This on-and-off character of the session is no doubt characteristic of this particular patient, but probably also holds out a more general lesson about the value of a fairly restrained, nonaggressive stance on the part of the therapist. He prefers not to pursue and confront the patient in order to break through his denials and resistances, thus avoiding a contamination of the transference by aggressive, sadomasochistic overtones. On the other hand, the therapist stays with the topics that promise to be related to conflicts that the patient is experiencing, rather than allowing him to run away from them completely.

The therapist thus follows the classical psychoanalytic technical principle of intervening to the least extent possible to ensure that productive therapeutic work is done.

SESSION 3

P. apologizes for not writing two stories he was supposed to write as part of the psychological testing, because he is "so hassled . . . getting very hassled again." Going to work and attending physical therapy really takes up so much time. Still, exercising is "a terrific idea" because he would never do it on his own, and he is heartened by the good example of others in the program. He is worried, however, that there is too much fat in his diet and he "would like somebody to take [him] by the hand and give [him] a list of foods and list of things that [he] should and shouldn't do." He recalls having suffered from "a nerve disease" in his late 20s which left him with a residual minor paralysis since he never went for physical therapy because he "got very pissed off at one of the doctors [he] was going to . . . he charged me $60 for a visit that lasted about 5 minutes, a neurologist. Of course [he did not do any therapy on his own but] when that happened [he] was a kid, and when you're a kid you don't care about things like that." This time he is trying to do better.

The therapist now reminds P. how, in the previous session, he mentioned some changes he would like to see in himself. Which would they be? What bothers P. most is his "lack of social contact with other people." He "never pick[s] up a telephone and call[s] somebody and say[s] let's get together." It is because he never feels "quite comfortable, confident and at ease . . . with a peer." He taught once and that was terrific, because he had "a fantastic relationship with kids . . . but that's with people younger than I am and not as life-experienced as I am, so I can be up front and they come to me for advice and professional help. With a peer, I never feel that confident." He feels "very unconfident" and inferior even with his best friend. He also has "trouble getting [his] own ideas across sometimes. (Therapist: You don't seem to have any difficulty here so far.) P. describes how his "major" client for over a decade reminds him of his father, and how "it took [him] about 7 or 8 years to realize that he reminded [him] of [his] father. And every time the guy would speak to me, I turned into a bubbling idiot." He was "very critical, extremely critical," would "get excited and start yelling." Recently, P. has been "a little stronger with him." He describes vaguely how yesterday he expressed his feelings to this man about a point of contention, but he still doesn't feel like he's "a peer of this person." The therapist asks how P. would have discussed such an issue with Dr. X. P. replies, after a pause, that Dr. X. told him that he goes through periods of depression, he "can't get [his] ass in gear, and he said 'You're like a man who's had the cork pulled out of his bottom' . . . and that's the way I feel generally." What brings these depressions about, the therapist asks? "Repressed anger," P. says, about being taken advantage of: by a nephew's girlfriend; by a cigar-smoking, drunken brute on a subway last week; by neighborhood organizations asking for favors, and so on. He recalls another incident with that major client in which he screamed back and as a result, got his bill paid sooner, but he "find[s] it hard to apply" that lesson. He recalls how, 20 years ago, "in really bad times [when he] was highly, highly neurotic [when his] legs became paralyzed, [he] couldn't drag [his] legs, was totally psychosomatic," his first psychologist "told [him] 'you don't walk around with your fly open, people can't see through your fly. They can't see through your pants' . . . it's a lot of sexual feelings with me. It's it looms up very big in my mind."

Th.:   You're telling about the present.

Pt.:   All the time. . . . For example, one time like, I told you I've had homosexual experiences. Uhm . . . I don't consider myself a homosexual. I prefer women, uh I've known a great deal, I'm not a social butterfly, but that's not my thing—but there's a lot of guilt attached to it.

Th.:   You mean the homosexual feelings.

Pt.:   Yeah, uhm.

Th.:   Do you want to talk about them. [Pause] or does it make you feel uncomfortable?

Pt.:   It makes you feel *very* uncomfortable. [Pause] I mean I feel like I have a secret life that nobody knows about.

Th.:   Do you ever talk about them, with anyone like Dr. X. or. . . .

Pt.:   Oh yeah um. . . .

Th.:   What did he say about it?

Pt.:   Well, he said you're not a homosexual and he didn't give too much importance to it. Um . . . this is an ongoing thing and . . .

Th.:   By ongoing you mean you still have some homosexual experiences?

Pt.:   Well, very rarely but it hasn't disappeared. Usually a disappointing experience . . . doesn't . . . I say . . . maybe it does fulfill a need, at a given moment, occasionally. Um . . . but I really feel uncomfortable about it.

P. recalls an incident when he was 11 or so, when his parents woke him up one night because "they had gone through my wallet and found this [obscene comic book] and they were hysterical . . . they did a real number on sexual guilt . . . [he was] young enough to make a scar." He doesn't act that way at all with his daughter. "She uses obscenity, and she talks about making out; my daughter's 7 years old." When he was a kid, he was a compulsive masturbator; he had to do it in the bathroom, in secret.

Umm, my daughter and I have started being a little more conservative. I, I like not wearing clothes in the house, particularly in the summertime. Uhm, and she occasionally makes a fuss about this, she was making a fuss but I started wearing undershorts around the house, generally, but I say if she walked in on me, I wasn't wearing anything, I wouldn't jump into the closet. Uhm, I kinda like that openness. Of course, it's not that simple . . . but I'm trying to [bring her up] without all this paranoia about sex. I think sex in this country disturbs me. I find it very fascinating. I think it's the most fucked up part of our culture. Uh, I'm having a lot of trouble with it now as I mentioned. I mean, I haven't gone out with women, since I, I went out couple of times since I split with my wife. I just haven't really made the effort and I feel really out of date. Uhm . . . I don't quite know how to deal with women now. I mean I have one woman friend who is a friend and we have been to bed several times in the past, but she's not, she's kinda frigid I think, and we're friends, you know, but I never make a woman, like some guys talk about this macho trip, and I really hate that kinda scene, but I don't quite know what the, what my place is with a woman. Uh . . . I get flirted with a lot by women.

When women do that, P. gets "somewhat embarrassed and don't know how to respond." He relates how a couple of years ago, a woman he just met professionally and was giving a ride to "asked me if I, what I think of extramarital affairs, and before I knew it, she was performing fellatio on me, I mean like, you know. The next day, her husband called me up, and I heard on the phone who it was, I [laughs] just about collapsed, but it was about business." He is "not unattractive to women, but I don't reach out. I don't take from people, I give, but I don't take. Uh, I never ask anybody for a favor." This is due, P. says, to two reasons: "lack of self-worth" and "to counteract that I think I want to feel so capable that I don't need anybody's help. . . . I have to prove myself all the time. I mean, my father thought I was, you know, just next to useless." His father was a mechanic, and "to him an artist was nothing," he was "very, very critical person, very stubborn . . . very uneducated, very limited scope." P. himself has a "hangup" about not "technically having a college degree," even though he is "better educated than a lot of college graduates."

Th.: Let me ask you, so far as were talking, this is the third time with me, how do you feel sitting here and talking with me, comfortable? Uncomfortable?

Pt.: Comfortable. In fact, I walked out last week and felt very high. I meant to tell you that. Umm I felt good, it's just it's a relief uh . . . of course, I haven't been going for any kind of therapy in a while and I don't know, my feeling is I'm not talking about what you want to hear because this is a crisis intervention center or whatever the terminology is and you're probably really interested in my reaction to having a heart attack, I guess, I don't know. Uh that's sort of fading as a, a, you know, it's not as big as it was last month. I don't have pains in my chest any more and it's [overlap]. . . . [inaudible]

Th.: Why do you think you felt so high when you left here last week? What do you think happened?

Pt.: I think the talking about homosexual, having had homosexual affairs, it weighs very heavy on me and letting it out to somebody that I think I can trust. My first wife, by the way, blackmailed me, because of that.

Th.: How do you mean?

Pt.: We had gone to a party one time with somebody from my office, that somebody in my office gave, who was married, but he was a homosexual and we had had some contact and at the party he got very drunk and his wife knew he was a homosexual, and we were the last ones to leave and there was something said, there was, anyway it came out between me and my first wife that I had homosexual experiences. I don't know if she knew it was with him or whatever. When we were, when we got divorced, she said you do everything exactly the way I want or I'll tell everybody that you're a homosexual. She's another bitch. And I gave her everything, and just walked away. I feel very vulnerable because if that's the word ah . . . I feel like, you know, if anybody finds out I could really, you know, it would be a disaster. Uh . . . you know people talk about these things much more openly. But I'm very uptight about it.

Th.:   Why, why do you think you're uptight about it? What do you think is bad about it?

Pt.:   Well, first of all, it is compulsive. Uhm it is not a thing that I'd go into with absolute comfort and joy and so on. Ah . . . so the fact that it is a compulsive act I think is bad. Uhm . . . my father would, you know, well, he would *kill* me. I mean he really would [overlap]. . . .

Th.:   You're still worried about how your father would think about you?

Pt.:   I guess so. Uh, I never said that before, but he couldn't deal with it at all.

Th.:   You think he was always right about everything he believed?

Pt.:   No, no I think he was rather ignorant. Stupid, he made a lot of errors about a lot of things. [Pause] I guess that must be it because, I feel like I'm in a cold sweat.

Th.:   Just saying that about your father?

Pt.:   Yeah, ooh. . . .

Th.:   Do you think there is something bad or wrong about saying something critical about your father?

Pt.:   Uhm . . . somewhat, yeah.

Th.:C Why?

Pt.:   Well he's dead.

Th.:   Therefore?

Pt.:   And, you know, I don't think you should, I should really, well I light candles you know, on, for Yahrzeit, my mother has to remind me but I do it and I feel the obligation to do it and when I do it, I say something for my father, you know. Uhm, even though he wasn't a particularly good father, he was my father and I think there's some care and affection that should be unquestioned.

Th.:   Does that mean you're not allowed to criticize him?

Pt.:   No, no . . . um, well, I never could.

He describes how on one occasion, when he talked over the phone with his father through his mother, because his father would never get on the phone himself, he got very angry when his father said P. wouldn't know how to do something, "and I screamed at my mother, you know 'Tell Dad to go fuck himself' or . . . something like that, which I never said, I never screamed at my parents like that, and after that my relationship with my parents changed somewhat. After that moment they pulled back, particularly my father. Uh, he died shortly after that." The patient "did not feel much grief . . . until way afterwards, a couple of years afterwards." He was in a group, on a weekend marathon. . ." and somebody mentioned their father . . . and it just started gushing out of me, Daddy, I love you, I love you. In retrospect, I feel very sorry for my father because he was so incapable of enjoying life." He still doesn't know if he feels guilty or responsible for his death.

Th.:   Why should you feel guilty?
Pt.:   Cause I screamed at him.
Th.:   Do you think that caused him to die?
Pt.:   No. . . . [long pause] At the moment I feel dizzy. I'm. . . .
Th.:   This must be very upsetting to you to talk about.
Pt.:   It is. [very long pause]

He hasn't talked much in a critical way about his father before. "The first years of therapy was always about my mother, cause I'm Jewish and I'm a boy; so I talk about my mother . . . I never, never even gave my father a thought" until that weekend. "Right after that [he] became impotent for about 6 months or 10 months while [he] was dealing with him!" He thinks his father withdrew from him when he was very, very young. He contrasts their lack of contact with his relationship with his daughter, in which they are "always hugging and kissing, touching. . . ." She massages my back for me, you know, there's a lot of contact." He wants to be a good father, he works hard at it and enjoys it. "I don't know if I'm doing right, but I don't know if anybody does."

Comment

P. begins this session with resistance—he did not write the two stories for the testing because he did not have the time due to physical therapy. As he continues talking about physical therapy, it seems that his comments, if not directed at, are at least representative of his attitude toward psychotherapy as well. He would like somebody to take him by the hand and give him a list of things he should and should not do; since he would never do what is necessary on his own, he needs somebody else to do it for him. But, if a person who is supposed to help him tries to take advantage of him (like the neurologist who charged him $60 for a 5-minute visit), P. will end up hurting himself (in that past instance by not going for the needed physical therapy).

Since P. seems to hint at wanting the therapist to tell him what to do, the therapist again redirects this question back to P. by asking which changes he had in mind when he spoke in the last session of the changes he would like to see in himself. The third time around, the answer is initially even more vague than before: "Lack of social contact with other people". But the therapist inquires further about this, and we learn that P. feels inferior and not at ease with his "peers." He can be "up front" only with people he is clearly above, like "kids" he taught at school. A question about how he discussed "such an issue" with Dr. X., reveals an abundance of homosexual-passive imagery (he can't get his "ass in gear"; he's had "the cork pulled out of his bottom".) We cannot know whether this was the flavor of what Dr. X. told him, but this is clearly how P. internalized it. He also recalls his first therapist reassuring him that he doesn't walk with his fly open, that people can't see through his fly, can't see through his pants. P. again mentions his homosexuality, or, as he prefers to call it, his "homosexual experiences," and his guilt about it. Since this is something P. mentioned before but only to run away from it, the therapist addresses this ambivalence by asking if P. wants to talk about it or does it make him feel uncomfortable? The patient says it makes him feel "*very* uncomfortable" but continues talking about how Dr. X. told him he is not a homosexual and didn't give too much importance to it. Yet, it still goes on. ("Well, very rarely, but it hasn't disappeared.") Repeating once again how uncomfortable he feels about it, he switches to talk of his parents "making a scar" on him for having a sexual comic book, and contrasts that with his "open" attitude toward his daughter. He reveals how he practically exposes himself to his daughter and of how women flirt with him. He says that he does not take advantage of that actively enough, but will submit to it. ("I don't take from people, I give.") Never asking for favors, has to do both with his "lack of self-worth" and need to prove himself in grandiose gestures—because his father considered him "next to useless." While once again being very evasive about his homosexuality, P. provides a rich contextual matrix for understanding it: feeling castrated by his parents for his sexual interests; being exhibitionistic toward his daughter, yet not knowing "how to deal with women" (just as he feels inferior and not at ease with his peers, but could feel terrific and be "up front" with "kids" he taught at school); feeling rejected by his father. When the therapist now asks about how he feels "sitting here and talking" with him, P. is comfortable and recalls feeling high after the last session, because he could "let out to somebody that [he] think[s] [he] can trust" about his homosexual affairs. He recalls his first wife sort of blackmailing him about it, and said how his father would have killed him. Yet, as he talks about these positive feelings about the therapy, he breaks into a cold sweat. Possibly, the occurrence of this symptomatic discharge while talking about his homosexuality and positive feelings toward the therapist resulted from P. experiencing a homosexual impulse toward the therapist, or a fear of such an impulse. A contributing factor to this reaction could also have been P.'s fear of being blackmailed by the therapist—a fear which may have been aroused by the fact that the sessions were being taped.

While the patient again spends much of the session talking in circles, these circles continue to encompass much meaningfully connected material. However, the therapist chooses not to actively pursue specific information which although interesting and ultimately important (for instance, when exactly did P. have his last homosexual experience, whom with, and what does he remember about it), is secondary to the primary goal at this point, that is, of obtaining meaningful data and doing therapeutic work without "contaminating" the transference with aggressive overtones.

SESSION 4

"I'm doped up with antihistamine." P. complains his allergy has been getting worse for the last couple of years. In addition, he has "been having a lot of trouble sleeping again." Last night, in the middle of the night, he had a pain in his anus that woke him up. During the night, when he's lying in bed, "little things become big things." He had this pain before, and he "really should have an examination, because colon cancer is fairly common." He is usually an optimist, but during the night he is always a pessimist: "If I have any bad feelings when I go to bed, that's it. I don't sleep." He wonders why he reacts so strongly to the nighttime: "I don't think I was ever traumatized at night, but, uh, because I'm not busy with other things, I think, I'm not occupied . . . and I think there is a chance for all the junk . . . to come forward in my mind. Actually, it was funny when I said I was never traumatized during the night." P. mentions how last week he recounted the embarrassing episode when his parents found a dirty joke book in his wallet. He recalls another incident when his parents telephoned one night that they would be late, and when they finally came home, his father was "half carrying my mother, she had fallen and her leg literally burst open . . . and I feigned sleep and didn't really know what happened until the morning." Without any pause, P. switches to say his brother told him he's "a real pain in the ass" because his wife keeps on bringing home names of women to fix him up with, but P. does not seem to be really interested. He replied to his brother that he is not, that his daughter is enough for the moment, but when he sees "a woman that looks like a nice, warm, friendly person, I get a little longing. I don't think you can live as a single person, alone. It just doesn't work. I think, you know, you actually need to have somebody." The therapist suggests that P.'s being alone could be connected with the way he feels at night, and P. agrees. He says he has a woman friend with whom he always hugs when they see one another, and how "it just feels so good, the physical contact, it's marvelous."

The therapist now asks how P. felt when he left the week before?

Pt.:   When I left here last week, I got lost. I become very disoriented very easily. . . . Well, instead of walking around [the usual] way I walked through the middle of the campus and I was sure I was walking in the right direction, and walked and walked. . . .

Th.:   Do you think it had something to do with what we were talking about?

Pt.:   Oh, yeah, yeah, I mean I walked out of here and I was, uh, totally confused, and my mind was off someplace. Uh, I hadn't thought about it afterward, it went out of my mind.

The therapist reminds P. how, in the previous session, he talked of feeling socially uncomfortable with other people, one of the reasons being that almost everbody he knows seems to be better educated. When asked if that also applies to P.'s brother, he replies that it does not, that education has nothing to do with the competition between the two of them. It was a "competition for my father, uh, because my brother was mechanical, more mechanical than I was; he was closer with my father." P. does not feel there was anything he could have done to have won out over his brother, but he won out with his mother; he was her favorite. Without any interlude, he says he has "a lot of questions on [his] mind about" his daughter. This is the day of the week that they part, and she got very upset this morning when he asked her to go to her nearby school by herself. "My daughter and I are very attached, very, very close, and I think we are too close." He describes how the previous night, his daughter refused to eat dinner at her friend's house so that she could eat with him instead: "We went out to dinner and had a very nice time. But she really looks to me for too much, I think, and I probably look to her for too much, because I'm alone. . . ." He is worried she does not have enough friends ("I'm oversensitive to that because I was like that when I was a kid and I don't want her to be undersocialized"). He is afraid that if anything happens to him, she would be devastated. He feels she likes him more than she likes her mother because her mother does not give as much warmth and affection to her as he does. He is also concerned that his wife may influence their daughter to become a lesbian, because she goes to feminist conferences and has a lot of lesbian friends. Yesterday, at dinner, his daughter told him that he really shouldn't hate lesbians because when she grows up, she might be one. So he feels he should be around "to present her with another part of the picture." He is not as worried about dying as right after the heart attack, but last night his pain in the rectum reminded him of an uncle who died precipitously of colon cancer. He had the pain a couple of times over the last 2 months. He procrastinates about going to a doctor; he does not particularly like doctors:

Th.: Why?

Pt.: Uhm [long pause] it's a funny thing, my, my mother told me a story a few years ago that my pediatrician used to try to fool around with her or something. Of course, to my mother, if he winked, that's a, a, you know, that's a sexual overture. Uh I don't know if that's the reason, but I just, I never go to doctors. I can go for years without going to a doctor. I don't believe in going and running to a doctor for every little thing.

Th.: But this apparently worries you?

Pt.: Yeah, I should have, well a proctologist is, is particularly the worst, I mean I particularly don't like going to a proctologist. I don't think anybody does. I've had a rectal examination once or maybe probably more than once, uh, uh a few years ago when I went for a general physical and that was really very uncomfortable.

P. abruptly switches to say he feels fine about his heart, although he sometimes worries about feeling too optimistic. The worst always happens, it seems to him, because he has had continuous disappointments. He waits till tomorrow, he puts off things, but "life goes by quicky and you have to do, you can't wait till tomorrow." This prompts the therapist to ask once again, what P. would like to do, to achieve, at this point. P. has to "make more money [but] it's not only making money, it's running my business successfully. I'm so disorganized." He talks about life insurance and his driver's license lapsing because of his negligence, of back taxes owed, of not being able to catch up with paperwork. He just does "not want to face" what he should do. He talks of one account he has had for years which represents 80% of his business. He knows that this is "a very dangerous position to be in. If I lose the account, I'm screwed. I should go out pitching other accounts, and I don't." (Why?) "Afraid of disappointment . . . I guess." Aggressiveness is what he really lacks.

Th.: Tell me, how do you think I can help you in this problem that you're talking about with acceptability, aggressiveness, how do you think you can be helped with those problems?

Pt.: I really don't think I can [overlap]. . . . I don't think I can change.

Th.:   Why? What makes you think that it's hopeless?

Pt.:   Because, I, I've gone through a lot of therapy. Uh . . . I've had optimistic periods in my life, when I could function better, but I always slip back into my old habits and ways of doing things. I don't think I'm gonna change.

Th.:   Do you think you don't want to change?

Pt.:   Uh . . . well I think the possibility of change, probably, I'm probably afraid of it.

He sounds as though he is afraid of being successful, the therapist says, and P. agrees, adding that "somebody once said to me there's a thing about not succeeding further than your father did."

Th.:   What do you think would happen to you if you should be successful, more so than your father? What do you think would happen?

Pt.:   You have to stand up and be counted to be successful. I've been able to get by by faking it. Now that's not quite true, I'm not, uh . . .,

Th.:   What do you mean actually?

Pt.:   My mother, when I was a kid, my mother built me up. She thought I was *terrific*. I couldn't possibly live up to her standards, her expectations. Uh . . . I have a, like for instance people have always thought that I was wealthy, wealthier than I am. Casual acquaintances. I don't, you know, this jacket is 10 years old, my pants have holes in it, you know, I'm not, I don't put up any front. Although I do put up somewhat of a front, a fake front, an image that is not partly, for instance my wife once said to me, "You know you think you walk around on tiptoe, but you really walk around in storm trooper boots."

Th.:   What did she mean by that?

Pt.:   Well, my wife and I used to have a lot of arguments, and I have a bad temper. When I blow up, I can really blow up. I scream and I throw furniture; I wreck the refrigerator [inaudible]. You know, I get very, very, very, angry. And I have the image that you know, I'm a mild-mannered pussy cat. When I was in group with Dr. X., there was a guy in the group that also said to me, one time, one time, I was wearing, winter time I usually wear boots. I don't anymore, and he once commented on my image of being such a macho, my macho image, you know. And the women in the group agreed with him, which really startled me. Now, I've heard, people said this to me before. I'm not macho, you know, I'm the furthest thing from it. I'm mush inside. I'm not a macho man.

Th.:   But you'd like to be?

Pt.:   I guess I would. I would like to be a macho man.

He goes on to say how he treats "every woman like a sister, like a daughter," he takes care, which means, for instance, that a couple of times he "wanted to get laid" and instead was "chauffering them around, treating them royally."

The therapist asks if he had not wanted his father to have had the great expectations of him that his mother had. P. "definitely" agrees.

Pt.: Well, I'm a male, a son and I wanted my father's affection, which I wasn't getting. My brother didn't get it either. He got some approval but my father couldn't give affection. He just didn't, he wasn't capable. Uh [long pause] I just lost myself. I have that feeling again that I get like low blood pressure and sort of faint [overlap] . . . .

Th.: Every time, when you talk about your father, that seems to happen to you.

Pt.: I also feel like crying.

Th.: Why? Why? what is it that makes you feel that way?

Pt.: Well, he's gone, there's nothing can be done anymore. Uh, I can't talk to him. My father and I never had heart-to-heart talks and it's like you know, it'll never happen, he's gone. He doesn't exist any more and he never knew that I wanted his affection. I could never tell him.

Th.: Do you think that you tend to look for people to make up for the loss, the lack that you missed from your father, that somebody who can give you the kind of love and affection that you never got from your father?

Pt.: Yeah, I told you my experience with my wife's grandfather and . . . Dr. X. I had a great deal of affection for, as did everybody else who knew him. He was that kind of a person.

Th.: How did he feel about you?

Pt.: He expressed concern . . . he was very warm towards me, even out of, off the couch. Uh, one time I was thinking of opening up an art store, and he's an artist, and he said, you know, after session come up to my apartment, let's talk about how it's really going to be nice to have an art store in the neighborhood and . . . and now it's unusual for a shrink/ patient relationship. Uh, I really appreciated that, I mean it was really, it was being treated like a peer of his rather than someone that was coming in with neurosis.

Th.: Like a friend.

Pt.: Yeah, uh. . . .

Th.: How do you think I compare with Dr. X.?

Pt.: Somewhat within the same uh realm. You have a very relaxed de-meanor which I like in people.

P. talks further about not being able to pace himself evenly in his work, and, as the session draws to a close, he worries that he is getting slowed down too much.

Comment

Themes of homosexuality and death, which appeared in the previous session (his father would kill him if he knew about it; P. breaks into a cold sweat just as he tells the therapist how pleasant it is to be able to talk to him about his homosexuality) continue into this session: a pain in his anus the previous night makes P. suspect colonic cancer and possible death. (An external threat—father—has now been internalized; is what happened ontogenetically being repeated in the progression of the therapy?) Associations are to feeling "traumatized" ("sexual guilt") by his parents, and of the (castration?) fears he hints at on seeing his mother with "her leg burst open." (Why didn't he ask his parents about it, instead of feigning sleep?) Further threat leads to P.'s feeling inept with women (he is "a real pain in the ass" because he does not try to date). The potential and unfavorable comparison with his brother's masculinity leads to thoughts of how he lost his father's love in the competition with his brother, as if implying that this is the cause of his lack of masculinity. This, in turn, leads to his admitting that he is "too close" with his daughter, and that he "looks to her for too much," similar to the relationship that existed between him and his mother. But instead of worrying about the effect that he may have on his daughter, or further, searching for related and probably unconscious incestuous feelings toward both his parents, he returns once more to blaming his wife for her influence on their daughter.

P. then returns to his "pain in the rectum" in order to pursue another line of associations: he procrastinates about going to a doctor, to a proctologist, because it is "very uncomfortable," and he recalls his mother and the pediatrician's "sexual passes." P. seems to be saying that he goes to a doctor for help, but exposes himself to being seduced and/or taken advantage of.

When the therapist asks how could he help him with "acceptability, aggressiveness" and so on, P. says he does not really think he can change. He always slips back into his old habits and ways of doing things. Further associations show that this is predictably related to his father's lack of affection and approval (which again brings feelings of faintness and crying) and, less predictably and maybe surprisingly, to the warm feelings toward Dr. X., who treated him like a peer and like a friend. Why feelings of being accepted by the therapist should have led the patient to the feeling that one cannot change, is not entirely clear, but seems to have been the case with P. and Dr. X. A partial clue may be provided by fears or fantasies of being anally, sexually penetrated and used by the doctor. Thus, P. would readily relate to a doctor the way he related to his father (docile, passive, submissive) and to his accidental, active-aggressive homosexual partners. Therefore, insofar as P.'s relationship to Dr. X. *repeated* both sets of feelings, that is, the rewards of feeling accepted and the punishments (benign patronizing) of these earlier passive, submissive encounters, rather than interpretively working them through, that therapy did not address these issues and P. had to give up any aspirations of "changing himself."

Related to this, there is the marked paranoid tendency in P. which helps explain why, on the one hand, he did not dare bring up such charged "relationship issues" to the therapist, and on the other hand, why Dr. X. deliberately avoided these same issues (e.g., You're not a homosexual"). This paranoia must also play a role in P.'s avoidance (so far, at least) of any of this treatment's major parameters (e.g., short-term and no fee, or the use of the tape recorder).

P. ends the session by likening the therapist's "relaxed demeanor" to that of Dr. X. as if to indicate further how much the transference conflicts with Dr. X are related to what P. is now experiencing with his current therapist.

SESSION 5

Th.: Did you have difficulty coming here today?

Pt.: No, no, no, I don't think so. I just have people working for me and I have to, if I'm out and I have to explain things to them, so I don't pay for them sitting there like this while I'm not in the office. Uh. . . .

Th.: How did you feel when you left here last week?

Pt.: Uh [pause] I don't, I don't remember. I'm feeling good now and when I'm feeling good, I put everything else out of my mind, I don't wanna know.

Th.: You were feeling good all week?

Pt.: Yeah, pretty good, well, it's springtime, this weather you can't, you have to feel good, you can't help it, it's cool, it's nice, it's sunny.

Th.: How have things been going for you?

Pt.: Uhm . . . good. I've gotten very busy all of a sudden, which always makes me feel better. Now I have work and . . . uh. . . . [pause] The only, the thing on my mind, I've been having trouble with my daughter . . . which I don't know, it's, it's kind of an involved thing, it's a long story. I'm having discipline, disciplinary problems, which I'm, disturb me somewhat. Uh, she frustrates me. You know, she won't listen to me. Uh, we end up sometimes having these little fights which I really don't like. I'm short-tempered, I lose my temper very easily and I run out of patience a lot, which I really don't like to do. You know, I see my wife performing exactly the way her mother did, doing all the dumb horrible things that her mother did to her and if I see any patterns in me that I don't like, I find it upsetting. Uh . . . obviously I do not have 100% control over everything I do, so. . . .

The therapist asks what P. sees in himself that he doesn't particularly like, and P. mentions his "impatience," and how he "started pulling guilt" on his daughter in an argument last week. They "straightened it out eventually, everything was fine," but he does not like that he dumps on her occasionally. He resembles his father in that, which he dislikes. He jumps at his daughter when she speaks slowly, mostly due to a slight physical handicap: "I don't have the patience. I cannot stand anyone who talks slowly." He tends to speed: "Before the heart attack, I used to race incredibly, could move three times faster than anybody else. Now I move only about one and a half times as fast. Uh, I still have a little bit of impatience with other people not moving fast enough." He is in a hurry to do things but he does not get a lot done: "My modus operandi stinks, my work style is terrible. . . . I do have a lot of frustration about getting older and not having done, you know, one-fourth the things I wanted to do." When the therapist asks him to name some of these "things," P. mentions only his lack of accomplishment in fine art. The therapist reminds him of how he mentioned last week that one of the reasons he was not more successful was that he was afraid to be more successful than his father. P. now somewhat ambivalently distances himself from that statement and talks about his father's story of how he could have been rich if he had only gone into partnership with a merchant who became rich: "It was so embarrassing, he sounded so ridiculous, [because] if you want to do something, you do it. You can't . . . you can't talk about it, you can't blame anybody else, you're, you're responsible for what you are and what you do . . . [pause] and I don't do much, you know, I, I, I just never get around to performing, you know, to doing." He has a fear of not performing up to his parents' standards. He is very competitive with himself. Fear of failure is holding him back. The therapist asks if it is fear of failure or fear of success, and again reminds P. that the week before he said that his father would not approve or like him if he were successful. P. replies, with a short laugh, that that must be so because he is "reacting physically . . . feeling nauseous." This discussion is making him uncomfortable and he has "a bad feeling coming up." "Nobody could do anything right" according to his father. His mother also "used to pull a number" on him by telling him "about the relatives, how successful their sons are. I mean, typical Jewish kind of thing. The lawyers, the doctors, you know," but she eventually stopped when he told her to. His mother probably wanted him to "be a prince, a Jewish princess prince, a male version of a Jewish princess." She thought he was "the handsomest, most wonderful, gifted person in the entire world. And that put a lot of pressure on [him] as a kid, to live up to her expectations. Uh . . . always found it embarrassing and painful when she would talk about [him] in front of [him] to other people, as parents tend to do." His father, on the other hand, "wanted [him] to be a mechanic . . . or something involved with the hard . . . hard goods, you know, something more concrete than a philosopher or an artist." His brother, who is an engineer, had "much more of a relationship" with father. Yet, P. likes using his hands, and is "pretty handy actually, not that much of a klutz." He would love to sculpt. He did paint and sculpt before, but not since he got married 10 years ago, since his apartment with his art work burned down. He is convinced his wife's carelessness was the cause of that fire. He is truly scared she might start a fire in her apartment and thus endanger his daughter. His wife was interested in his art work, but was "so fucked up." At one point when he got fed up with his business, she offered to support him if he quit and started painting full-time. But, he "didn't take her up on it . . . [because he] could never live under that kind of situation . . . that would be an emasculation . . . cause then she'd turn around and say, you know, 'you're no fucking good, you never made enough money,' so . . . that would have never worked." He would love to make his living as a pottery maker. He should at least do it as a hobby—but he does not because he has to be the expert in anything he is in: "Everything I do, I have to, I have to succeed at, and I have to feel like the other people around me look up to me as the expert . . . and when I don't feel that way, when I get into something I feel inept, which there are things I'm not trained in, obviously, uh, I hate being in that position. I hate being a junior." He recalls how when he taught for a while he loved it, "absolutely *basked* in it, it was like being in the sunshine, or being upstage, it really was a terrific feeling," because that was a situation in which he was the expert. He realizes that this keeps him from doing anything that he does not feel like an expert in. The therapist remarks about how P. sounds similar to the way he described his father to be. "That's right, that's exactly it, exactly. [Pause] That son-of-a-bitch. [Laughs] I hate him. Uh . . . that's right, absolutely right. [Pause] Uh, I'm even dogmatic the way he is, was." He describes how he would get his point across to his students that their pencils should be properly sharpened, "if I saw any kid working with an unproperly sharpened pencil, I'd go around, pick it up and snap it . . . my father would have done exactly the same thing." He was rigid, but, "in the last couple of years [he has] become sloppier and . . ."

Th.: [Interrupts] So you've changed.
Pt.: Yeah. [Long pause] Sometimes I get very good feelings about myself. Like right now I have a very good feeling about myself.
Th.: At this particular moment?
Pt.: Yeah.
Th.: What do you think is the reason for it?
Pt.: I feel a relief, uh I think I just realized that I have changed, that I'm not as rigid as my father. Uh, and that I've mellowed somewhat over the last few years, which is good. That I'm not *really* that much like him.

Th.:   That you don't have to be like him.
Pt.:   That I don't have to be like him, I'm not like him. It's funny, you know, it's, it's a little painful. I, I think uh, uh you know he's such a fucking bastard that, I get angry very easily so that it gushes out. Uh, one of the things that, that I've heard other people express too in their relations with their parents, if somebody dies off and you never told, you never, you never have a chance to tell them and that pisses me off, and it's his fault and that, that, you know, I have a pain now, I'm talking about a guy who fucked me over and it brings up pain instead of anger, uhm, which he's not entitled to. Uh, you know, I could have given him love, I had a lot to give and he wasn't able to accept it or to give it and that was his hangup and it makes me angry now that I feel pain when I think about it. Uh, you know he left without saying goodbye, is what happened and you know, that's it, and there's no way of ever finishing that situation.
Th.:   (Overlap) What would you have. . . .
Pt.:   It's real, well, I wanted to tell him that I love him and I wanted him to say that he loved me which he never, ever did, ever.

His "fucking [wife] is the same way" as his father, he continues, and he fears she is not able to give their daughter any love. Her own parents are like that—"nice people, but ice-cold, I hate people like that." He thinks his daughter will hate her mother in a couple of years when she gets older. He is concerned his wife gives her wrong, confusing messages by exposing her to her lesbian and militant feminist friends. He wishes there was a woman in his life who could be a model for his daughter.

Comment

After coming late, and failing to address this adequately, P. starts by complaining about how he "has to explain," has to give detailed instructions to "people working for him," or else he "pays for them sitting there like this." This is, possibly, an important clue about thoughts P. may be having about therapy. He has not, so far, openly addressed either his feelings about the fact that this treatment is free, nor has he commented about how he feels it has been going so far. When the therapist tries to look for possible associations to the previous session, P. "does not remember." He feels better, apparently primarily because he again has (more) work. Yet, as he complains about his daughter, he repeatedly mentions his impatience with other people not moving fast enough, not talking fast enough. While these comments cannot be taken with absolute certainty as being indicative of how P. experiences the therapy and the therapist's style, the absence of any direct or veiled comments on these issues by P. makes us suspect that these statements have a direct transference meaning. The following sessions should provide some clue to what extent this is so.

As the session proceeds, P. traces his impatient, rushing style to his dissatisfaction with his achievements in life. But just as he was repeatedly vague in all the previous sessions about what he would like to accomplish in the therapy, so too he is vague here about things he feels he missed out on: "accomplishment in fine art." When the therapist reminds him of a statement from the previous session that he was afraid of being more successful than his father, P. berates his father for talking about what he "could have been." But, in the same breath, P. talks of his own inability to do things, to perform. Thus he clearly identifies with his father's shortcomings, but does not comment on this specifically. The therapist's reminder of P.'s comments the week before about how his father would have disapproved of his success, brings P. to report he is "reacting physically" by "getting nauseous."[3] He again talks of how his mother did him harm by her unrealistic expectations of him, but does not recognize how much he still craves exactly what she expected of him, witness his talk later in the session of how he stays away from all endeavors in which other people around him do not "look up to [him] as an expert." From his comments about his parents' expectations of him, we must assume that he experienced them both as emasculating—mother's driving him toward being effeminate ("Jewish princess"); father's expectations reinforcing his experience of castration. However, his identification with father's castrating attitude is not too far from the surface. The therapist's interpretation, "you sound the way you describe your father was," brings P.'s immediate recognition and an additional example of his identification with his father's castrating attitude (i.e., breaking his students' pencils for being "unproperly sharpened"). The therapist's encouraging comment that P. has changed brings a dramatic alteration in P.'s mood in the direction of a positive, upbeat quality. He seems ready to forego insights just arrived at in favor of an optimistic, "positive thinking," upbeat bit of deception ("I'm not *really* that much like him"), when the therapist's further correcting remark ("You don't have to be like him") allows him to feel supported. In this optimistic position, he continues analyzing his relationship to his father, frankly recognizing his unfulfilled wishes

---

[3] Perhaps this nauseous feeling is a bodily response to the therapist's more confrontive style at this point in the session. Thus the patient reacts physically, rather than verbally, to the therapist's not allowing him to get away by "safe" but meaningless generalities. This physical reactivity to emotional stress was also noted earlier when the patient broke out in a sweat when talking about his homosexuality.

with respect to him. He ends the session, however, by again villifying his wife, seeming unaware that it is possibly more a case of his attitude toward her being like the attitude *he* had toward his father, than her being actually "the same way" as his father.

SESSION 6

P. comes to the session 20 minutes late.

Th.:   Sit down. What happened?
Pt.:   I was dealing with someone who was moving very slowly and I didn't reserve a car at the car service. They didn't have a car and I got all fucked up.
Th.:   Do you think there's some other reason why . . . .
Pt.:   [overlap] No, I don't think so, uhm, I don't, I don't think there's any hanky panky on my part. . . .
Th.:   How did you feel after the last session last week?
Pt.:   Uhm [long pause] I can't remember, I always, lately, any time I talk about my father, I walk out of here feeling kind of exhausted.
Th.:   Uh huh.
Pt.:   Uh . . . I can't really remember any specific . . . .
Th.:   How have you been feeling this past week?

He felt "up and down"; he "was very pissed off" that he keeps letting it happen, that he spent the holiday weekend practically alone: "I should be involved with other people." He feels "inactive." He even let his apartment "go to pot" while before he "kept it so clean, you could eat off the floor."

> I haven't done anything. Yet I can't get myself rolling. I just, I'm obsessed with, with not having contact with people. I need a woman, and you know, I put it out of my mind, uh I try to tell myself I don't need anybody, you know, it's all over, but any time I do meet somebody, you know casual, just talk to, to, particularly to a woman, you know the longing just really comes up.

He blames it on the lack of opportunities. Besides, he is "waiting . . . for things to happen instead of being aggressive and going out and getting them to happen." Also, he has "a fear of being discovered . . . that I'm not what I appear to be. [Which means what?] not very aggressive, masculine." P. recalls how his first wife knew he had "homosexual experiences" and "blackmailed" him: "If I didn't give her everything exactly the way she wanted, she would tell everybody." His present wife "also knows about it, which I'm sorry that she does." P. feels she "never gave it much importance." He recalls how when they were first married, he "really wanted to do some sexual experimentation, but she couldn't handle it at all and the whole thing was dropped." He reveals "a fantasy" to make love to two women at the same time.

Th.: Have you ever done that?

Pt.: No. Uh . . . actually I don't know if I could really handle it. You know, it's, it's not an intellectual play. Uh, that brings up something I haven't discussed with you, and I haven't because to really explain it, is so involved, so complicated.

Th.: Why don't you try?

Pt.: All right. I've been having an affair with my wife's sister.

Th.: Wife's sister, what . . . .

Pt.: Now that's a setup right away, obviously, for guilt and all kinds of disrupting things, uh, I haven't seen her in a year but we've talked occasionally and we felt we will get together *again and again and again*, same-time-next-year kind of thing. It's the most beautiful affair I've ever had. It's just incredible.

P. recounts when and how they first got involved when she was barely a teenager.

Pt.: Yeah, well it started out, you know, uh . . . intercourse didn't happen for a couple of years afterwards, but we played around, and had oral sex. When I was in group with Dr. X, I had a slight nervous breakdown, a mild nervous breakdown a few years ago and I think she was the reason.

Th.: Well, what did it consist of, this breakdown?

Pt.: Well, one day I was walking in the street with [my wife] and I just became hysterical, for no apparent reason, and I couldn't cope with anything. I went to bed, I remained in bed about a week. Couldn't handle anything at all. I couldn't eat, I couldn't, total disruption of my functions.

He told ("spilled it") in group therapy, what had happened and the women in the group "wanted to throw [him] out the window." But he feels they eventually admitted that his affair with his sister-in-law was "very beautiful."

Pt.: [She] was never traumatized, you know, it wasn't that kind of thing. Uh, it was always so incredibly beautiful that, I mean, for having that affair, it's the kind of thing that very rarely happens.

Th.: Why do you think it led to your breakdown?

Pt.: Well, the tension that it produced, uh . . . I mean [she] would spend time at our house and every chance we were in each other's arms and we would make love and so on. . . .

A couple of years ago, she stayed at their house for a few weeks and they "made love on an average of three times a day; it was just incredible, you know, just the sexiest, most sensual woman I've ever met."

P. intersperses his story with criticisms of his wife's behavior and attitudes, as if implying that she was responsible for his starting the affair: "after [our daughter] was born, she got lead in her ass, or something, she just lost her 'joie de vivre.' . . . . During the summer, I really hate sitting in in the evening [and she] would never go out; she spent all her time on the phone . . . she preferred to talk on the telephone to her girl friends." He thinks his wife does not know they were "actually lovers," although she "of course was very pissed off" about the two of them going out and spending so much time together: "Dr. X. told me she doesn't know because we've both been going to him for a while."

P. now calls his wife's next (female) therapist "another whore" because she confided her own marital infidelity to her patients:

> This is a therapist talking to a patient, which I think is really fucked up. And it speaks of where the women, the intellectually free women in my neighborhood are, they're really fucked up. . . . I mean I was thinking of going to [another neighborhood] to find myself a nice Jewish girl because the women in my immediate circle, in my large group, uh . . . . I don't think they're worth shit. The last couple of years I think they, they've all gone off the deep end, and they're so fucked up they don't know what they want or what anything is about. They're just, they're so strange.

As P. continues criticizing women, the therapist "refer[s] to some of the things [they] talked about last week" and asks P. if his fear of being criticized is not related to his seeking the friendship of older men, like Dr. X. or the therapist himself:

Th.: Somebody who can take the place of the kind of father that you really didn't think you had.

Pt.: Yeah, I, definitely uh [long pause] I'm not going to get that, you know, that fulfillment.

Th.: How would you describe the men with whom you've had homosexual relationships? What kind of men were they?

Pt.: I'm not, I'm not talking about any kind of real relationships, you know, it's, I mean most of the time we don't even know each other's names, it's nothing. Ah . . . I don't, I don't relate to them at all. I don't, you know, I've never had a, a, an affair . . . and actually I'm, I'm passive, you know.

Th.: Do you get picked up usually?

Pt.: Well, there are, there pla, yeah, yeah. I'm not gonna act as a partner. Uh I've never had a homosexual affair.

The therapist asks P. what he got out of the affair with his sister-in-law, and P. vaguely mentions "enjoying life," and says how a year ago, the last time they spoke:

Pt.: She said, "Do you realize I've lived out my oedipus complex or desire, whatever," which I had thought about all along on her part, but she had never realized she wasn't.

Th.: What do you think she meant by that?

Pt.: Well, her father is the same way my father was. Uh, he's an ice-cold guy. I like him, actually he's, as a person, but he never shows any emotions.

Th.: She had the kind of relation with you that she. . . .

Pt.: Would have wanted to have with her father. I think that's really laid out there. What effect it would have on her 20 years hence, I don't know, what effect it's had on her. I don't think it's had any. Uh, she has steady boyfriends, you know, we have a very, very unique special kind of thing. Uh, in relating her to the fulfillment of the father role, I don't know. Uh, it was just very, very enjoyable.

"She was able to accept a lot of love from me and she was able to give a lot of love," P. says, and contrasts that with the fact that he and his wife were not having much sex in the last few years and were "not turning each other on at all."

Pt.: . . . masturbating or having intercourse with her, it was like floodgates opening and water trickling out, and I really thought it was all over, I mean, I thought I'm getting older and that's what it is, but then when I had sex with [sister-in-law] it was orgasms down to my fingernails, it was just so incredible.

Th.: Did you think of marrying her?

Pt.: We talked about getting married eventually. Uh, she talked about it seriously and I always thought, well, you know uh, by the time she's ready to get married the age difference will be ridiculous. It's out of the question. Uh I mean we talked about it, you know what would happen at Passover, could we invite her parents, you know, they would be my in-laws twice over. Nah, that's out of the question. Ah, but I think you know, I don't know what will happen. I don't talk to her for months at a time. In fact I saw her about a year ago.

Almost in the same breath, P. expresses contradictory opinions: that their relationship "will fade" and that "it will just go on like that . . . same time again next year, same time"; that he "is not a playboy," does not like being dishonest and that he "had a one-night stand with two other women while I was married. Uh, one . . . both of them were aggressive towards me. If they hadn't instigated the event, it wouldn't have occurred." The session ends with P. rationalizing his affair by saying that his sister-in-law's age was conducive to it because he was older and more experienced than she and therefore did not feel threatened by her.

Comment

P. comes very late but rushes to deny any "hanky-panky" on his part. Instead, he blames it once again on "someone moving very slowly"—a possible unconscious allusion to the therapist. Thus P. may be showing impatience with the success of his own game of bringing up conflictual issues but not addressing them fully, as if expecting the therapist to do that for him. Similarly, P.'s self-criticism regarding his inadequacy and inactivity in respect to women ("waiting for things to happen instead of going out and getting them to happen") can be understood as a wish in the transference—that is, he would like to address his desires and conflicts openly vis-à-vis the therapist, but not knowing how to do this, he reacts with impatience and frustration, again, as if expecting the therapist to do it for him.

Early in the session, P. admits to his affair with his teen-age sister-in-law. He idealizes that relationship, minimizing and denying the possible effects it had on the two of them. The moment he mentions that Dr. X. betrayed his wife's confidence by telling him she did not know of his affair, P. becomes enraged at his wife's second therapist for confiding to her patients about her own affairs. He then wipes the floor with women in his neighborhood ("they're worth shit . . . fucked up . . . so strange.") The therapist apparently senses that the vociferousness of this attack may have to with P.'s guilt about his affair, and asks about the relationship between P.'s fear of being criticized and his seeking the friendship of Dr. X. or the present therapist. P. says that he is "not going to get that fulfillment." The therapist makes use of this to suggest that what P. seeks in homosexual encounters is related to the wish for a kindly father, and asks P. to describe his homosexual partners. P. is very vague, and with great discomfort says how these are not affairs, but anonymous encounters at "places." P.'s difficulty apparently makes the therapist uncomfortable enough to stop pursuing further elaboration of this. For the rest of the session, P. once again glorifies his affair with his sister-in-law, and practically accuses the only two other women with whom he had "one-night stands" as having "instigated the event." ("If they hadn't . . . it wouldn't have occurred.")

SESSION 7

P. comes 15 minutes early.

Th.: You came early today?
Pt.: Well, I have to get a car, car service. Uhm . . . last week, when I, I, when I left here, I ca . . . I got [pause] when I left here last week uh very, very depressed, really went downhill, very, very rapidly.
Th.: Do you know why?
Pt.: Uh [pause] Not quite. I was, I think I wasn't feeling well. I don't know, I can't even remember now. When I was walking home from the office and walking up my block, I just, I felt like I was gonna die very suddenly. Uh I felt like right there I, I, my daughter wasn't with me, she was at her mother's house, uh I felt as if right in the street, I was it was just gonna stop, it was all gonna end right there and uh I felt like there was no purpose in doing anything.

As he walked up to his building and exchanged a few words with some kids having a stoop sale, one of them told him he has no personality and suggested he buy his. P. said, with a laugh, how he "wanted to go back and kill him."

Th.: Do you remember what we talked about that seemed to have upset you that much?
Pt.: Can't remember at all. I know it was about my father, I can't remember specifically.
Th.: [overlap] Every time we talk about your father, it seems to have a bad effect on you.
Pt.: Every time. [pause] Uh [pause] how much, any specific uh. . . .
Th.: Some of the things you were talking about had to do with the feeling that you had that you have difficulty relating to other people, both men and women because you feel as though you're not aggressive enough. You don't have sufficient aggression . . . do you know . . . what that stems from?
Pt.: [overlap] Yeah. Before we get into that, I want to mention something else. I was having lunch, I usually eat alone because I just run down from my office and grab something and the guy that I'm somewhat friendly with that lives in my building walked in and sat at my table and we were talking and sometimes when I talk, my throat just clams up. It, like it goes into spasm and my voice sounds funny and I said to him, "Does my voice sound funny?" and he said "Yeah, you sound very distant." It's a thing that's been happening more and more lately. Uh when I was talking last week, you had the air conditioner on, making a lot of noise and I'm very hypersensitive to noise and I was like pushing my voice to talk. Uh I guess it's just kind of an obvious thing, when I'm in

an uncomfortable position, or I don't feel like talking I guess, my throat really gets very, very tight and lately it's been, it's been like that a lot. Uh I feel like I'm withdrawing more and more.

After some generalities and a few pointed questions from the therapist, P. says that what made him uneasy about that man was his suggestion to do something together with him, like go to the theater. "The only thing" that comes to P.'s mind about why this should be uncomfortable is that he "will feel inadequate" and be "found [to be] lacking." He guesses that comes from "the old man": "I could never do anything right by him."

Th.:   How have you felt now that you've been sitting here talking with me over this period?
Pt.:   You mean, about you personally?
Th.:   Mm. . . .
Pt.:   Uh [long pause] comfortable. I don't relate you to my father. [Very long pause] When I, I never told you when I met, met my ex-wife's grandfather it had a profound effect on me because he reminded me of my father but he was a person with some warmth. Uh that was very direct but you know, men in general uh. . . . I like you. You have a relaxed demeanor which I like in people.
Th.:   Haven't you found other men who have relaxed demeanors that you've been with on occasion?
Pt.:   Yeah, yeah, but uh I always, well I always feel that I have to prove myself, or something of that nature.
Th.:   By proving yourself, you mean what specifically?
Pt.:   [long pause] Well having enough knowledge, or whatever we're talking about, I have to have the knowledge.
Th.:   You mean being better than they are?
Pt.:   No.
Th.:   More than they are?
Pt.:   Either as much or more. If I know less, then I really feel uncomfortable. Uh [very long pause]. . . .
Th.:   Does it work the same way when you're with a woman?

No, he does not feel the same way with a woman as he feels with a man: "I feel more valid with a woman. Uh, I don't feel inferior." He "noticed this before, this is nothing new and my feeling is that women are a little bit more sensitive than men and I don't have much in common with a lot of men. Uh, I'm not in the stock market, I'm not into sports, I'm not into aggression, bullying, whatever." He should not be in business, but an artist. He never went in for that because of . . ." fear of failure. Uh, my mother used to inflate anything I did so huge that I hated it. I mean, you know, the compliments were so, were laid on so heavy." He feels his father was not that absolutely against his being an artist ("he would have accepted it if I was successful"), but he certainly was not encouraging. P. recalls how in college he used to "freeze up" (he mentions in an off-handed remark that he froze when he had to draw on the psychological test after the first session). He dropped out in his final year after a teacher embarrassed him in front of everybody for plagiarizing an ad for his homework assignment. When the therapist reminds P. that his father once asked him to copy art work for him, P. replies:

Pt.: That's right. Wh, you really do your homework.
Th.: You seem surprised that I remember what you say.
Pt.: Well, you remember things that I forget and when you say them of course I remember them. [pause] Well how do we get rid of my father, now? Uh, I'm kind of amazed that, I mean I've been through a lot of therapy and he's the one now.
Th.: You never really talked much about your father?
Pt.: Not a great deal. Uh somewhat. Uh you know, I mentioned that when I was in group, never talked about [mumble] all of a sudden I'm just regurgitating. Uh [pause] I wish I had done this 20 years ago.
Th.: Do you think it's too late?
Pt.: I think it's kinda late.

He mentions fear of dying soon, but also his feeling that he could enjoy life only if he "really changed, but I don't think I could change any more, I just, I think I've lost that flexibility." He mentions having worries and flashes of his daughter getting hit by a car, and that he "may be thinking of her as an encumberance." Yet, if not for her, he "would have committed suicide a long time ago." P. says he had problems lately with flatulence, and talks of an idea to write a book on the subject which he feels "could sell" but, he will never do it because he never takes such ideas any place. The evenings his daughter stays with him, she takes up all the time, and when she is not there, he is depressed. Another reason he is not working on that idea for a book is that he does not trust his judgment. Sometimes he wonders if "maybe I'm really a nut like one of these vagrants" on the subway who talk to themselves. Other people do not invite him to parties or to their house for dinner. "Maybe I see myself as somebody that I'm not, as somebody else." However, P. dilutes this thought by talking about how his cultural and other tastes are so different. He mentions again how he often does not respond to advances by women.

Th.: Why is that, do you think?
Pt.: [long pause] I really . . . I, I really don't know. Uh you know what I

want to say is they got teeth down there that bite. Uh . . . I don't think I trust women.

Th.:   Why? What do you think they would do to you?

Pt.:   I have a, a, I had a fantasy several years ago. I don't know whether it was a dream, or a semi-dreaming state, and what I was doing was shooting a film and I was getting married and my wife and I, it was my first wife, were standing in this room with a rabbi standing in front of us and there was a table in front of us and the bride reached over, unzipped my fly, and took my penis out and laid it across the table and then the rabbi turned into a butcher with a meat cleaver and just went zap and chopped it off [laughing] kind of [overlap]. . . .

Th.:   But it was the man who did it not the woman who castrated you. What do you think [overlap]. . . .

Pt.:   I never even thought of that.

Th.:   What, what comes to your mind when you think about the dream or fantasy?

Pt.:   [pause] Well, the man has to be my father, and the woman, my mother.

Th.:   What do you think it means?

Pt.:   [laughs] Jesus Christ uh [pause] Well, my mother set me up for the kill, allowed it to happen.

Th.:   Do you think—what it seems to me is that your father may have resented your closeness with your mother.

Pt.:   Yeah, my father was a possessive person.

Th.:   Uh huh.

Pt.:   Uh you know, there musta been some hidden jealousy of my relations with my mother.

Th.:   Have you ever noticed it, observed it over the years while you were with your parents?

Pt.:   No [long pause] No, nothing specific. [long pause] My mother told me after my father. . . . several years after my father died that, you know, how different things are today. If they were this way when she was young, she would have left my father. He was a very difficult man to get along with. [long pause] Well that interpretation of that scene . . . never occurred to me.

Th.:   What did, what did you think of when you first thought of it?

Pt.:   Well, something more immediate, which is both my wives are bitches.

Th.:   Uh huh, uh and they were the ones who destroyed you.

Pt.:   Yeah, uh well of course that fact that the man is one that's doing the emasculating, I just never thought of it. [long pause] My mother is a heavy woman . . . when she was younger, when I was younger, she was really obese, fat. Uh and we used to sometimes we'd cuddle together, she had great flabby arms, they were very soft and I used to love to lay my head on her arm. [mumbles] I don't know why I said that, what I was thinking of. My daughter and I are like that and I really don't think that it's good.

He recalls that his brother reminded him of how he drew two figures of naked women on the wall when he was 7 years old. He was "sexually

precocious, the first one in my group to reach puberty and start masturbating," which was always done in secret. He "always felt embar-
rassment about my own sexual, my own sexuality."

Pt.:   How do I get cured. I want to stop this crap and start living. You know,
         I feel like all I have to do is go out and do it, but somehow. . . .
Th.:   Something stops you.
Pt.:   Every time. I just c . . . can't work.
Th.:   I'm afraid we'll have to stop now, but I think we should talk more about
         it.

Comment

Instead of being late as he was to the previous two sessions, P. comes
15 minutes early. He starts by saying he left the previous session
feeling very depressed. He does not remember what upset him so
much in the previous session, but guesses (somewhat inaccurately) it
was his father. When the therapist asks for a more specific response, P.
says he would like to mention something else first. He talks of
"straining his voice" when talking to another man and compares this
with his discomfort when talking during the session last week. While
he attributes the discomfort with the man to the fear that he will be
found inadequate and lacking, (which "comes from his old man"), it has
much more to do with the homosexual wish/fear activated by this
man's offer to go out with P. (to the theater, where P. already had
indicated he took women with whom he really wanted to "get laid").
Thus P. once again throws light on the main lines of the current edition
of his conflict. Feelings of inadequacy, both with women and socially,
are connected with feeling castrated, abused, and abandoned by his
father; he attempts to compensate by establishing sublimated, pas-
sive-dependent relations with men (currently with the therapist).
However, openly homosexual impulses keep breaking through and
cause P. to panic. The therapist gingerly tries to make this transference explicit at this point, and asks P. about feelings toward himself.
Once again, the therapist elicits only relatively generalized positive
transference expressions: P. feels "comfortable," he "likes" the therapist and his "relaxed demeanor."

The tone of the session changes somewhat when P. becomes genu-
inely surprised and happy that the therapist remembered something
he had said a few sessions ago and, feeling protected by the therapist's
concern, exclaims "Well, how do we get rid of my father, now?" A little
later, toward the end of the session, he comes up with a castration
dream-fantasy and appears quite surprised when the therapist points
out it was the man, not the woman, who actually castrated him. This
brings some additional memories—of how his mother told him a few

years ago, how she would have left his father if the social climate was what it is now, and how he did feel physically attracted to his mother. It also brings another burst of "therapeutic enthusiasm" at the end of the session: "How do I get cured? I want to stop this crap and start living."

SESSION 8

P. starts by informing the therapist he "hasn't slept in three nights" and goes on to describe sleeping difficulties and increased "feelings of alienation" and "detachment" even when he's with others: for example, he had lunch with his mother and other family members—he "had hard time talking to her"; he "grabbed all the checks and paid them all [even though] it wasn't necessary." During a dinner with friends, he "couldn't relate at all—felt like shit."

The therapist asks, "Do you think this has something to do with what we've been talking about? How did you feel after our last meeting last week?" P. recalls walking out of the session "physically drained" and somewhat misidentifies his father as the subject of the session; he talks more of his disorientation. The therapist reminds him of the castration fantasy from the last session and tries, with a few pointed questions, to elicit the patient's thoughts about how that fantasy may be related to his difficulties in relationships with both men and women. The patient reponds by becoming flustered, almost agitated and blocked: "I don't know. I can't think."

Th.:   Is there something on your mind right now that's upsetting you? Just being here and my asking you these questions? Does that bother you?

Pt.:   One thing occurred to me the other day is that I don't know how many times I've been here, but if this is a short-term program, it's starting to worry me.

Th.:   [overlap] Well, what is it that worries you about it?

Pt.:   Well, I can't afford, I'm, I'm very tight, I can't afford to go back into therapy. Uh and I'm afraid that, you know, like 3 months is gonna, is going to come, the end is gonna come very soon.

Th.:   How do you feel about that?

Pt.:   I find it very upsetting because uh . . . I'm getting into stuff . . . or the process that is going on is a little heavy for me and gee I'm afraid I'm gonna be left holding the bag, so to speak of, you know. Uh I've been let down in the past and it's gonna end . . . I . . . you know, it's a little scary.

P. goes on to talk about recent dreams in which his father appeared and he interpreted one of them to mean that "going through this stuff about my father [in therapy] is earthshaking or, hopefully, will produce a great change, a realignment of things." The therapist then reminds P. of his concern that therapy "is about halfway through and you're worried about what will happen when we're finished."

P. replies that he "knows it's not a 10-minute deal" (something he never hinted at in all the previous sessions!) and starts talking of "mixed feelings" regarding further therapy, because of his "difficult" and "uncertain" financial situation. He goes on talking about a "client from the medical field [who] coerced [him] into doing some thinking without getting paid for it" but the therapist again refocuses him on the transference issue by asking about similarities between that doctor who exploited him and this therapist who got him into something but will soon leave him. P. weakly denies any anger at the therapist but in the same breath says he's going to be angry when the therapy is over because "I can't push it all back down, it's too late" and "you're not a philanthropist." P. again talks about his social isolation and withdrawal, and fears his daughter will find him "lacking" because of that, especially because his wife is socially active. As his comments become more and more depressed ("It just seems worse than ever and getting worse . . . I really want to go away . . . into myself and away from everything"), the therapist again inquires about the patient's experience of their relationship and therapy. P. pauses for a second, then says he feels "like smashing something."

Th.: Do you think you're angry with me and would like to smash me at this point?

Pt.: Yeah.

Th.: Why?

Pt.: I don't know, the only thing I can think of is because of what you've drawn out.

Th.: And because I'm going to eventually let you down?

Pt.: Well, you're going to go away in three 3 [pause-banging—mumbles something like] very, very angry.

Th.: Do you think in a way that you may have been angry with your father when he died, that he left you.

Pt.: Yeah, I uh, that came up way, way afterwards, uh, when he died I didn't feel anything or very little, but years afterwards, I started feeling that er I was very pissed that, that he died. Uh you know the thing that everybody feels when somebody dies, you can never ever again say anything, or deal with them.

Th.: You really had strong feelings for him.

Pt.: It's funny, I, I, brings up an enormous amount of pain. I can't remember any, uh I mean I've seen pictures of him holding me when I was a kid, when I was a little kid, but I can't remember ever being held by him. Uh . . . I can't remember him being affectionate.

Th.: That's what makes you angry with him, that he wasn't as affectionate toward you as you wanted him to be.

Pt.: He wasn't at all, just.

P. spends the remaining few minutes recalling his early and later experiences of his father, the family atmosphere, and events from the time he was three to 5 years old. His major regret is that, for all its shortcomings, his family, which meant a lot to him, is now "all gone." ("There's no family, there's nothing. Nothing is left, its all been, its all been destroyed and I want to go back.") Finally, he recalls, but can only begin to associate to a dream populated with family and other figures from the time he was 3 to 5 years old.

Comment

P. begins this session by building a case that he's worse, not better; he's unable to continue exploring a central castration fantasy from the last session even when reminded of it. The therapist correctly inquires at this point about the here-and-now transference issues and this brings a statement from the patient about his anger at the shortness of the treatment. He even hints that the therapist may have wanted to lure him into long-term and financially burdensome therapy by offering free sessions first. However, the therapist continues to raise and interpret transference issues and the patient responds. He begins to articulate negative transference feelings and misgivings about the shortness of the therapy. Although these negative thoughts were hitherto unmentioned, and presumably at least partly unconscious, they have now clearly reached an explosive level.

Unexpressed, these feelings led to acting out, feeling worse, and having difficulty working in the sessions. Unaddressed, they would have crippled or even aborted the treatment. Although the patient clearly had great difficulty expressing these thoughts appropriately, the therapist's initial facilitating questions and comments enable the patient to initiate their expression first, in an accusatory, paranoid form. However, with further interpretative work and repeated re-focusing, the patient is not only able to formulate and express these feelings more fully and integratedly, but also recalls and better grasps aspects of his relationship with his father and relates these to his current problems. He thus starts the work of better understanding both genetic and present material, the exploration of each helping the patient to understand the other better.

SESSION 9

P. says he has "a terrible hangover" and relates in an almost casual manner how he "went to a friend's house last night" and how the two of them "ended up finishing almost 2 liters of wine." However, he got "really smashed" and, reaching his home, dropped his keys down the elevator shaft, so he "had to go back to [friend's] house and sleep on his couch." However, moments later, when answering a query about why he did this last night, patient suddenly changes his tone: "I thoroughly enjoyed it [laughs] but there is another problem . . . [pause] . . . I'm falling to pieces." He starts complaining he's "forgetting everything" and "fucking up [his] work." The pitch of his complaints increases ("I'm so disorganized . . . in the last few weeks, it's getting worse and worse").

Pt.: I have to function, you know. . . .
Th.: What do you think it is that causes you to . . .
Pt.: Well, I'm very upset [cries] this stuff I'm working on, it's ripping me to shreds.
Th.: I see you're crying now.
Pt.: I can't er . . .
Th.: What is it particularly that's upsetting you so much, do you think? What is it that we've been talking about that's been so . . .
Pt.: Well, my father.
Th.: Yes.
Pt.: I'm just dizzy.
Th.: You feel dizzy?
Pt.: [sighs . . . pause] I had the shakes this morning, uh which is probably from drinking actually. But I also got the shakes when I'm very nervous [sighs . . . long pause].
Th.: What is it about your father that we've been talking about that you think is so disturbing?
Pt.: [overlap] I'm a scream, I can't, I can't do any more [sobs] . . .
Th.: You can't do what any more?
Pt.: I don't wanna, I don't wanna bring up any more stuff.
Th.: Uhuh, do you think that . . .
Pt.: I'm so angry, you know, and it's wrecking me. I can't . . .
Th.: What are you angry about do you think?
Pt.: [sigh . . . sniff . . . long breaths, inhales and exhales loudly] I feel like I'm losing control. [sniff]

He starts talking about a photograph of his father holding him and switches to how he got in touch with a new lawyer to finalize his divorce. Yet, he doesn't want to do that: "I don't know what to do, I'm going crazy, I don't know what to do with myself and I want my wife back . . . you know, I hate her, but the idea of, er, really finalizing is very unpleasant though." He continues talking about feeling badly.

Th.: Remember what we talked about last week?
Pt.: I can't remember, you know I have this feeling, first of all it feels like I was here yesterday. I have no sense of passage of time and I know that I went home and was thinking about it and I wanted to tell you things [cries] I can't remember, whatever it is, I can't remember. [sighs] Jesus, I feel so fuckin' lousy.
Th.: Would you like a glass of water?
Pt.: No, I can't afford to feel like this. Uh [pause] there's a lot of work in the house [laughs] and I, I can't get it out. I have so much responsibility.
Th.: What do you think it is that's on your mind that keeps you from doing your work?
Pt.: [Cries] I'm afraid, I'm afraid of this therapy.
Th.: What are you afraid of?
Pt.: Something's gonna happen.
Th.: Like what?
Pt.: Something's gonna come up that I don't want to come up I think.
Th.: Can you think of what it might be?
Pt.: I, I really have a feeling that something, when I was very, very young. I have on my scrotum, I have a seam on the bottom of my scrotum and all during childhood, I thought that nobody told me but that I must have been split in half and it was sewn back together. I since realized that that's a natural thing.

The patient then interrupts his recollection of how his family used to fight a lot to say he "feels like breaking those windows, you know, I, I feel like jumping out of the windows."

Th.: You must be angry, you must be angry with me. As you said last week you remember that here we are talking about these very, very upsetting things and in a while, well you can consider it to be in a short while, this program will be over and where will you be is what you're worried about. You felt very angry with me for it, do you recall that?
Pt.: Well, yeah I am afraid of that, I mean I'm just not gonna be able to stop, not like this. I'm gonna have to continue therapy. Uh which pisses me a little bit because I'm, I'm, I have two more payments on one of my bank loans. I'm so anxious to finish it and get out of debt. You know, I'm trying not to spend money, you know, because financial is, is a problem, it's only a material problem, but you know it just aggravates things.

The patient goes on to say how he did not take his heart medication yesterday and today, how he is depressed, "fucking up at work" to the point that it's "intrinsically dangerous."

Th.: I think what you're saying to me is that here you are upset and I'm responsible for it because I've been responsible for your talking about, thinking about all these upsetting things and in a while I'm going to dump you and therefore, you're in terrible shape, and I can't possibly do that to you, is what I think you're really saying to yourself.

Pt.: Well, let me ask you is it possible for you to take me on as a patient after this is over? I, I know I'm going to need therapy, I can't you know . . .

Th.: We can talk about that later, we still have some time left. This is as I told you at the beginning, this particular program is a short-term program.

Pt.: I know, see I feel, I, I, it must be very obvious to you I've been through a lot of therapy but something's going on now which had never gone on before.

The patient tries to explain what is different this time: The therapist ("You know, a psychiatrist's technique is kind of an abstract, subtle thing"); the fact that he's "working more on my father"; and, "the scare of having a heart attack" makes him "much more aware of myself, you know, much more aware of your vulnerability, of your mortality!" He says that the therapist is "getting to him," reminds him of his father ("physically, a little"). Otherwise he finds the therapist different from his father and "very, very easy, spontaneous, easy going, relaxed, which I find it very nice to deal with a person of that nature." He switches to say he treated himself the other day to a nice dinner, had a lot of wine, started to feel angry that he was alone, and deliberately snapped the wine glass in his hand. He talks of his ambivalence toward women. He wants them and yet he does not, because "they are all whores, or they're lesbians or they're fucked up." He talks of feeling out of place at a West Side party where he was taken by a younger woman with whom he was sporadically involved.

I'll, I'll tell you something happened last night that I really don't want to but maybe I should. I ran out of clean underwear yesterday and I was wearing a pair of women's underwear that ended up in my laundry in my apartment house, I found in my laundry one time. [laughs] When I went home and I dropped my keys, I went down the basement, I tried to find the super and I was, I was wobbling, I mean I was really drunk and then I figured, well I have to go back, I have to go back to Frank's house, I'll sleep there and then there's this whole shit. I'm wearing a pair of women's shor . . . underwear, I can't go there cause I'll take my pants off, you know it would be rididulous. So I went into the laundry room and I started wrestling trying to rip them off me. It was, I got, I almost strangled myself trying to get these briefs off and I think I put the light off, I'm not even sure, you know, people might have seen me or something. Then I got, I went to Frank's house and I realized that Frank and I once had a conversation and he said something about having sex with a man at one time. He said, "Did you ever try it?" I said, "No." Then last night, he has another friend—that he just split with his friend—ah he makes it with guys once in a while [inaudible] like nothing. I mean a lotta guys this happens to and its not such a deep thing. You know, but I'm, oh when I went back, I told them that I was wearing these briefs and I had to take them off because I . . . uh, you know, I mean that alone is in my mind so much bigger than. . . .

He grew up feeling that "homosexual was one of the worst possible things that you could be," and recounts a number of "exhibitionistic" episodes in which he would masturbate in view of others, from early adolescence through his first marriage. After a silence, he says:

Pt.:   I feel like saying to you "I want to commit suicide."
Th.:   Why?
Pt.:   Because what I want is help.
Th.:   Do you feel you're not getting it?
Pt.:   Yeah, I feel like I'm getting it, but I need a lot, I need a lot of help.

P. then admits he's "being dramatic"; when therapist asks him how he thinks his daughter would feel if he killed himself, P. starts crying: "It would destroy her"; when asked how his wife would feel: "she don't give a shit. I'm sure she'd cry, but I could kill her." When asked how he thinks the therapist would feel, he laughs, "Well you certainly wouldn't feel good about it." The session is about to end, and the therapist suggests to him he can rest for a while after the session before leaving, which he accepts. He expresses the feeling he "would really like to go away now and just leave everything." The therapist concludes "including me . . . [If] I were going to leave you, you would rather leave me first."

Comment

Pt. starts the session very similarly to the previous one, by talking of how terrible he feels and how poorly he functions. The main purpose of this is to induce the therapist to continue seeing him. However, his tone is much less paranoid—accusatory—and much more openly depressed. In this context, he states his ambivalence about his wife, and links his current frustrations with childhood feelings of being unloved by his father. In response to one of the therapist's repeated interpretations, he is finally able to state his purpose openly and maturely. He asks the therapist if he could see him as a private patient after the short-term program is over. Even though he does not get satisfaction on that point, the therapeutic alliance appears to be strong enough to permit the patient to proceed with the therapeutic work on a mature and appropriate level. Thus he talks more of his ambivalence toward women, and then returns to the incident from the previous night that he could only mention at the beginning of the session, and then only to misrepresent and cover up its real content. Now he related it in such a way that homosexual tendencies become obvious (although the patient cannot fully acknowledge them for what they are nor relate their up-surge to the feeling of being abandoned by the therapist–father). He does further work by bringing up his related exhibitionistic tendencies. However, possibly under the impact of the session coming to a close, he again yearns for a more dynamically primitive interaction with the therapist: "I feel like saying to you I want to commit suicide." This, however, is expressed in a form which is at a much higher and more controlled level than all of the earlier self-destructive acting out, and most likely reflects the therapeutic work that has been accomplished to this point. In effect, he is saying, "I am commiting slow suicide by messing up my work and my life." Not only can he now acknowledge the primitive means he employs so as to induce guilt in the therapist ("I want to commit suicide") but he now replaces action by words. As such, he distances himself from the act and has an inkling of its relational (transferential) meaning: *"I feel like saying to you I want to commit suicide."*

The therapist, on his part, continues to interpret, but also, by an open show of concern for the patient's suffering, offers him minor help which has elements of transference gratification: he offers him a glass of water and gives him permission to rest in the area adjoining his office after the session.

SESSION 10

P. called a half hour before his appointment and left a message that he could not come. Then he called again, around the time of his appointment and told the therapist that he got delayed and asked if they could reschedule the appointment for the next day. The therapist agreed.

P. starts to explain that he was "with a client in the city and we were involved in a very, very complicated situation, I couldn't leave. . . . I felt very bad about missing an appointment, obviously, I don't want to miss appointments, so I called back." He had no idea he would not be able to return on time because he left "very early in the morning" for the meeting with his single most important client. However, "it dragged on and on [and I] had a huge, huge fight with the client, a screaming, raging, cursing fight." The conflict was caused by his "dysfunctioning" and not getting his work done. "I was very, very late with the job. It didn't come out too good." Besides, he was "totally exhausted," so when the client "started bitching" he "just couldn't hold it in." It was all really the client's fault because "he insisted on doing something in a cheap way which couldn't be done . . . instead of 20 hours' work, it took 100, literally 100 hours' work to do something because he wanted me to do it cheap and I'm not gonna get paid for all that. . . ."

The therapist asks why he undertook the work when he knew in advance he couldn't do it like that. P. replies that he lets himself be pushed, he always accepts things. He agrees with the therapist that he finds it hard to say no, and explains he wants to be considered important, wants to "be a hero." He gives an example of how he wants to help young neighborhood artists who "always come up to me for advice." He does it free but he "can't spare the time, it's crazy." P. then clarifies, once again, the sequence of calls that he made the day before. He asked for another appointment only at his client's encouragement, because he "felt out of place asking if you could rearrange the appointment" when it's free.

Th.:   Do you think it had something to do with our session last week when you were so upset and agitated when you were here, do you remember that? And angry with me?

Pt.:   Well, the thought crossed my, my mind, that I wanted to grab your lapels and shake you. Uh, I had been thinking whether this, all this pays or not, whether this process is working. Uh, before I came here, I wasn't functioning too well. Since I started, it's gotten worse, but I wasn't too happy before either, so I think it's worth it. I mean I, whatever happens, I imagine it'll get better. Gee, I always have a lot of thoughts after the session, but I can never remember them. [overlap] I have a terrible problem remembering them.

Th.:   How have you been feeling since our last session last week?

Pt.:   Uh, I've been kind of busy, which I don't feel anything when I'm very, very, I'm working very hard. I've become totally preoccupied.

He goes on to complain of his mother-in-law ignoring him and goes on to put down his wife and all the women in her family—mother, grandmother, sister—as "tramps" and "really fucked up." He mentions the age at which they "lost [their respective] virginity" as proof of that. Following a long pause, the therapist mentions the date of their last session. P. says it makes him feel like throwing up. This feeling reminded him of a fellow group therapy member who started throwing up, severely and uncontrollably, when talking about his mother (she "used to shave his legs when he was a kid and he went swimming so he shouldn't look ugly. The guy was really fucked over by his mother . . ."). He felt "somewhat the same way" last week or the week before and when he thought about it after the session. The therapist reminds him that he "sort of recalled last week that it had something to do with when you were a child and you thought it involved your mother and your father fighting and maybe your father taking a knife and wanting to stab your mother or something along those lines." P. confirms this, saying it is very vague in his mind. He's been "thinking of sitting down and talking to her, er, I don't know if she can handle it, or if I can handle it. . . ." He reports conflicting feelings of not wanting to bring it up, just wanting to get rid of it, and also feeling "kind of ridiculous talking about something that I don't know what it is. . . ." He mentions having a fantasy as "a kid" that maybe he was adopted; he recalls his "grandmother and aunt who were always screaming and fighting, uh, and my father and mother used to, used to fight a lot." He switches, with no interruption, to talk of how his daughter used to crawl into bed with him in the morning until she was 5, and how recently, on account of hot weather, she spent two nights in a row in his bed and he thinks "that's not a good idea . . . but I'm always afraid of this reaching out to her for a little bit too much, but she reaches out to me a lot, too. [long pause] When I was younger, uh, something about when I used to shower, I'd insist on somebody drying me. My mother used to dry me after I showered." He thinks his reason for that "must have been sexual." He compares himself and his daughter ("I think I was much more sexually mature than she is") but then contradicts himself, saying she is "aware":

Pt.:   When I was a kid, it was all in the dark, with guilt, and I got, I think I got sexual guilt when I was like 7 to 8 years old.
Th.:   What were you guilty about, do you remember?
Pt.:   Uh, well, I know it had to do with my mother. I saw my mother nude.

He recalls drawing nude fat women when he was 7, masturbating ("I was the first on my block"). He stops pursuing this, says he's "kind of tired."

Th.:   Too tired to think and talk about yourself?
Pt.:   Well, I would like to. I'd like to get some work done. Uh, but I don't feel much like today for some reason, which I'm very disappointed about. . . .
Th.:   Do you think it had something to do with the fact that we're coming closer to the end of the program? What do you think about that?

Pt.:   Uh, maybe I'm starting to turn it off. That's upsetting me. It's, I want to change my life. I'd like to pick up this chair right now, smash it, smash it.

Th.:   On whom?

Pt.:   Well, just on the floor. Not on you.

Th.:   Why do you feel so angry right now, do you think?

Pt.:   Uh, 'cause I'm getting fucked, you know, the session's gonna end, the process ends and . . . I'm in a limbo. . . .

Th.:   . . . Remember you talked last week about how I resembled your father in a number of ways. Do you feel that in a while I will be leaving you the same way your father left you when he died? I think it makes you feel angry.

Pt.:   Uh, yeah, yeah, I'm not angry, I'm dizzy . . . [long pause] Well, I don't know what I can do about it except to accomplish something in the session. . . .

P. talks about how the client he had the fight with is really a nice person, that he reminds him much of his father, but is better because after a fight with him he feels better, unlike with his father, who would just clam up—"he never gave me a chance to say anything . . . never expressed feelings, never argued a point." What he "absolutely" misses is that his father never showed him affection. He feels angry about that now. He recalls another "horrendous fight" between his parents but remembers it very dimly. Recalling how he slept for a while at his grandmother's house, he remembers that must have been the time when his brother had his appendix taken out—that "might have been a traumatic thing."

Comment

In an inspired combination of acting out and acting in, P. has a big fight with a father-like business client and thereby makes it impossible to come to his session on time. He also forces the therapist to choose between two unpalatable alternatives: One was *not* to make up the session. With a clearly decompensating patient, this would have made it easier for the patient to disengage from the therapy and cast the therapist as a rejecting, punishing figure. In a long-term intensive psychotherapy, this would clearly be the preferable alternative, because there would be plenty of time to interpret and work through the patient's misconstruals. However, with just a few sessions remaining, the alternative seemed more sensible. That is, to gratify the patient and "make up" the missed session. This move probably also had a symbolic meaning to the patient; that is, of quasi-magically negating or qualifying the main fact which was disturbing him—the impending end of the treatment. Despite a potentially seductive effect of such a "gift" from the therapist, it was considered to be the more appropriate alternative here in short-term treatment because it helped stem the malignant self-destructive reaction of the patient, and reinforced the working alliance with him. Incidentally, it would have been appropriate and fully consistent with the overall treatment approach had the therapist actively confronted and interpreted the transference meaning of this acting out. He, however, elected not to pursue that avenue, preferring to allow the patient to achieve a more stable if less thorough or perfect balance in the face of the approaching abandonment with the end of treatment in sight.

In the session itself, P. comes across as much more stable than in the previous two sessions. He is depressed, and feels empty and insecure, but stops actively and self-destructively trying to get the therapist to keep him in therapy beyond the contractual 14 sessions. ("Well, I don't know what I can do about it except to accomplish something in the session . . ."). However, he does not explore his feelings about the ending as openly as he does in the forthcoming sessions.

It is interesting to observe the, by now, almost typical relation between the main transference theme of the session and the content of what the patient chooses to talk about: faced with abandonment by the father-therapist, and in a depressed mood, P. talks viciously of women with whom he was sexually involved (his wife, even his teen-age sister-in-law), reminisces freely about incestuous impulses toward his mother and his daughter, and then gives us another clue about how these two themes are related by recalling a (screen) memory of a "horrendous fight" between father and mother, being away from the parental home (at grandmother's home), and his older brother being away because his appendix was taken out. Themes of separation and abandonment by an omnipotent father and incestuous and aggressive impulses toward women are connected by a screen memory of a primal scene (fight), by fear of abandonment (not being home), and by a castration threat (brother's appendectomy).

SESSION 11

Pt. comes late to the session: "I apologize, actually a friend of mine called me who is in the same situation . . . [and] I couldn't get him off the phone. In the same breath, P. switches to talk about how his mother called him just after the last session, and he asked her about the events that occurred when he was 2 to 3 years old. For one, his grandfather died and he and his mother were sleeping at his grandmother's place. For another, his brother had his appendix taken out. But "the really big thing was that my father had left the family." While his mother didn't say if they had actually separated, she did say that his father left when he was 3 years, 10 months old and did not either write or call them. Immediately preceding his father's departure, they had a lot of financial problems and fights in the family; they could not pay the rent (which P. connects with his brother having an operation), so they went to live with the maternal grandmother. Eight months later, his mother took the patient and his brother to Ohio, where they stayed with her brother. They were looking for the father. One day, shortly after P.'s fifth birthday, they drove to a place where they knew he was. The patient expressed surprise that he did not have more of an emotional reaction on hearing about it. He's sure he "missed him or felt the separation," but, on the other hand, he "knew he was away for a while but I had no idea for how long and I'd really forgotten about him."

P. interspersed these recollections with worries about how his daughter is too clinging, and didn't want him to leave her when he took her to school that morning; how he took her as usual, to the park where they jog, but this time they played ball. His daughter, being a "klutz" like himself, did not do well and he criticized her, which made her not want to play any more. He recalled that his father, in such situations, "would make you feel like shit." P. was clumsy and would get hurt when playing in the school. This reminds him of news that his mother gave him about his brother's life-threatening medical condition. This upsets and scares him. His mother also told him she would like to maintain a relationship with his ex-wife, so that she could have access to her granddaughter if something happens to him. This unnerved the patient a little. He then asks when the last session will be, because he's planning a vacation. The therapist asks if he's been thinking about termination? "Umm, no, it hasn't been upsetting for some reason." His mood vacillates, and at the moment he feels like he has stepped over a hurdle. He feels there must be something else other than his father leaving that upset him in his childhood, but does not know what it is. Then he states that his father, like himself, never reached his potential.

Pt.:   I don't feel very emotional today.
Th.:   By that you mean what?
Pt.:   Well, I er, I can get in touch with my feelings fairly easily and I, I just feel like I'm rambling and not talking about anything really. Uh, time's valuable.

Th.:   Do you think it has something to do with the fact that in a while this will be over and I'll be leaving and why should you talk about things that are very important and significant if I'm not going to be here to talk to you about them.

Pt.:   Umm, I don't know, it might be the opposite, that I feel in a rush to take advantage of the situation. Uh, I don't know, I think I feel good.

He relates this "feeling good" to the friend who made him come late today and his inviting him and his daughter for a barbecue and the fact that he was supportive and encouraging about P.'s conflict with his wife: "I told him I went to a lawyer last week and he said, 'Oh, I'm really glad to hear that, it really makes me happy that you did that,' and I had that feeling it's nice for somebody to talk to you with concern." However, he'll "have to shell out two and one half grand for the goddam lawyer which makes [him] angry." But he feels he needs "a real son of a bitch" that this lawyer is, because his ex-wife has been "screwing him out" of the money that belongs to him. He switches to talk about his vacation with his daughter and how his mother is pushing to go with them, too. He goes on about this until the therapist interrupts:

Th.:   You're trying to find things to talk about, is that it?

Pt.:   Yeah, I think I'm I'm. . . .

Th.:   You're blocking.

Pt.:   I'm blocking? Maybe I am trying to separate myself. I feel like I'm not talking really truthfully. I'm kinda chattering cosmetically.

Th.:   Last week you talked about how angry you felt with me, you felt like grabbing my lapels. Do you remember when you talked about throwing the chair through the window. How have you been feeling about me since last week?

Pt.:   I don't know. I have good feelings. I don't feel that anger right now. I don't know if I'm blocking or what, I, I'm not feeling any particularly strong feeling at all. You see, anger is the easiest thing for me to express, uh, and I think it could be very easily used as a coverup. I may cover up for. . .

Th.:   What?

Pt.:   Dealing with something else that's more important or or maybe painful.

Th.:   Like warm, friendly feelings.

Pt.:   Yeah, yeah and that's yeah. I er, er I'm very s . . . sarcastic, I love to put down uh.

He goes on to say how he puts down "an incredibly beautiful" young girl working for him, for her liking pop music, even though he really thinks well of her, and how he drives people off, does not maintain friendships ("I never call anybody, I never reach out . . . I have to be dying to call somebody") and always feels uncomfortable with people. He talks of not being able to extricate himself from a conversation with a neighbor, even though he was in a hurry to get to his office. The therapist inquires about how P. feels "sitting here with me now." P. reasserts that he feels comfortable, that he can say what's on his mind, and adds how he has stronger feelings about memories when he talks about them "in here" than with other people. The only thing he still feels uptight about talking of is in "the sexual area." He then recalls many tics and compulsions he had as a child and later. Before this therapy he used to rehearse things before actually saying them. He worries about his "halitosis" and how he may be driving people away on purpose.

Comment

Pt. again comes late, although less so than in the previous session. He "couldn't get a friend off the phone," but his later statement about that conversation ("I had that feeling it's nice for somebody to talk to you with concern") explains better why the patient preferred staying on the phone to coming on time. He reports gaps in his childhood memory that his mother filled in with her information. Interestingly, P. intersperses the story about his father leaving the family and his uncertainty about father's return with worries about his daughter's overdependence on him and his inadequacies with her, as well as with worries about the possibility of his brother and even himself dying. Finally, he asks when is the last session. But when the therapist openly inquires about termination fears, P. denies it is upsetting him. And, indeed, the tone of the session is entirely different from that of sessions 8 and 9, and even session 10—although the quieter moments of that session herald this one. However, P. unwittingly suggests how his peace of mind has been achieved: "I don't feel emotional today. . . . I've been busy, I don't think, I just run." Coming late has to be understood in this context, in which P. is trying to distance himself from the therapy, saying, in effect, "What I do out there, whether business or social, takes precedence." The flow of his associations clearly connects termination with abandonment by father, brother's appendix being taken out, and even death. The therapist asks a few direct questions aimed at facilitating P.'s expression of these fears, but he largely ignores them and the therapist leaves it at that. He has two reasons for doing so: first, the extent of the patient's exasperation in the previous three sessions and, second, the fact that the patient is able to continue with the therapeutic work, putting together pieces of his history with his present life experience. Although he does so somewhat haphazardly, his analytic work preceeds in a productive way.

SESSION 12

"The only thing that could happen this week is, I'm feeling sexual frustration. Women in summertime turn me on. The way they dress, it's terrible." The patient goes on to bemoan his lack of initiative despite "an awful lot of smiles" he gets from women in the street. He regretfully compares this with the behavior of a "rather stupid-looking guy" on the subway who approached two different women and got polite and "nice" responses from them (even though they both left the train with this man still on it). Similarly, he feels "like a shmuck" when he sees women, who work on a neighborhood magazine, go to a movie: "Here they are in a group of 2, 3, 4, 5, you know, walking down the street laughing, kidding around, and there I am going to the movies alone." When asked what holds him back, he "can't quite figure it out. To say that I hate women I think is ridiculous." He thinks it has to do with his ex-wife and "the finding of her in bed with another guy." This still seems to have left a lingering impact, "a permanent scar. . . . Before I was married, I didn't quite feel this way. I wasn't this immobilized. But, I was always not the most aggressive person, but I mean, I used to go out and get laid occasionally, more than occasionally. But, since I've separated from my wife, uh, nothing, you know, I just, uh, it's over a year already. It seems to me it should have dissipated. It should have been over, uh, but it's not."

He mentions that his daughter told him that the man he found in his wife's bed visited her the other day, and that he had a response "uh, that shmuck," and that it still gets him upset. When the therapist reminds him that he has, for a long time, been having an affair with his wife's sister, P. replies "It doesn't count . . . because it is an emotional-reaction, it's not an intellectual reaction. . . . Intellectually, I believe that we should all have the right to sleep with whomever we want to. But emotionally, it doesn't work that way. . . ." Sensing an underlying dynamic, the therapist asks P. if he may have been jealous of his wife for having a relationship with this man? P. denies this, saying he was jealous of her "social success . . . her jumping back into life quicker than I did. You know, there's a whole network for single women that they have very well structured." He goes on to say that the other day, he had a dream which had a lot of impact. He "can't remember it now, but it had to do with his wife being a lesbian." In addition to his wife and his daughter, there was this female friend of his wife's in the dream who is "an asshole" and whom he suspects of being a lesbian. "I think my wife may be gay, I'm not sure." Therapist asks about the dream, but P. just says "it was very complicated." He is worried that his daughter "is going to get fucked up signals" from his wife. His daughter sometimes does not want to leave him to go to her mother, and this makes him angry because it means she is not a good mother and he does not feel he can raise a daughter by himself. He feels that his wife "doesn't pay much attention" to their daughter. He recalls an episode from the last week when his wife brought their daughter to him for the weekend. He had planned to take his daughter to a barbecue on the roof of his friend's house. He was dining in a restaurant, had already "finished off half a bottle of wine and was just a little tipsy, but I was very upset and I can't quite remember why. . . . [They] walked in and I was a little agitated, and my wife said, 'I don't want you taking her up on the roof, it's too dangerous.' So I said 'Don't worry, if I jump off, I won't take her with me.'" Although his wife angrily left at that, she called the restaurant 5 minutes later "to see if I'm all right" and then called him later at home. When the therapist asks P. what he thought of "her great concern" about him that day, P. evades acknowledging her concern, denies feeling really suicidal, and admits it was an attempt to make her feel guilty. "I would really like to do something to hurt her. I'd like to slap her in the face . . . just whack her across the face . . . I don't hit people, I never have in my life. Uhm [laughs] but I'd really like to do it." He recalls an embarrassing incident when he "started strangling a girl." They were 11 or 12, and he used to walk this girl home, and they would "neck a little bit, we'd kiss" and there was "one real fruitcake in the class, real faggy kind of mesomorphic lump, couldn't stand him," who would follow them. P. got very angry at him once "and started shaking him and I had forgotten to take my yarmulke off so this girl reached up and grabbed the yarmulke and I turned around and I grabbed her throat." At this point, the therapist again brings up the dream of his wife being a lesbian, asking if he remembered how he felt during the dream, pleasant or unpleasant? "Very unpleasant," he says, and again switches the subject, saying that once, in group therapy, he defended a lesbian's right to raise her daughter. He goes on to say that the downfall of his marriage was "partially my fault also. . . . I didn't fulfill the role that I should have. My nonaggressiveness is the ruination of a lot of things, uh, wishy-washy."

Th.:   Since you're aware of it, why do you think you find it so hard to do it, be more decisive?
Pt.:   Well, it's standing up, being counted, making demands, I can't make demands. Uh, I don't feel I'm entitled to make demands of other people.

Th.:   Why? What do you think you've done that makes you feel as though you're unable or incapable or haven't got the right to make demands?

Pt.:   I don't know. I just don't feel valid.

Th.:   You've used that word other times in the past. What do you mean being "valid"?

Pt.:   [overlap] Yeah. Well worthwhile, important. I feel like I'm kind of, you know, worthless, amorphic, nothingness. I feel almost like I'm not there. Sometimes. Uh, I just don't exist.

Th.:   But you know you're important to a number of people, certainly you're important to your daughter.

Pt.:   Yeah, until she sees through me, is one of the fears I have.

Th.:   What will she see if she sees through you?

Pt.:   She said the other day, relative to something, I forgot what it was, "you have no friends" and it's quite embarrassing coming from her.

Th.:   Is that true.

Pt.:   Well, it's, it's er, yeah. I mean I have a couple of acquaintances but I don't have much interaction. You know there hasn't been anybody in my apartment except my daughter and I for months, and months, and months. . . . My daughter is used to her mother going out on dates, you know, and I never do. I haven't had a baby-sitter, 8 months and I think she wonders why. Why there are no women in my life.

He is worried that "as she gets older, she'll see my problem more. You know, kids think their father is 10-feet tall. My fear is, as she gets older, not only will I come down to 6 feet, but I may start shrinking, shrinking, shrinking." He goes on to complain about insomnia.

Th.:   Do you think it might have something to do with the fact that you're approaching the end of this program 2 weeks from today?

Pt.:   Uhm, if it does nothing is registering about it. Uh, I have no con . . . I haven't thought about it. No conscious thoughts. I think what I, what I possibly have done is that I wanted to think that the thing I discovered about my father was it, period. And now that I know that, I'm cured.

Th.:   It doesn't work that way?

Pt.:   [laughs] No I guess not. Uh but I think I, I kind of turned off or built up a block, you know, a wall, er not wanting to dig further or not wanting to start anything because it's coming to an end. Whatever the reason, I'm, I'm ice-cold. [pause] You know, in fact, I feel totally, I think ice-cold is the term.

Th.:   By ice-cold you mean. . . .

Pt.:   Very unemotional. Well, I say, I, I, I, you know I get emotional at the drop of a pin. I've stopped. You've had it with me, that's it.

Th.:   So you feel you don't want to open up anything that may cause you any kind of upset or distress since we're not going to be continuing beyond 2 weeks from today, so why should you start anything new.

Pt.:   That may be it, that but I'm only guessing, because I don't, I didn't think of it consciously. Again, as I said the last couple of weeks, I'm busy, so that kind of takes care of a lot of stuff. I don't have to bother living if I'm busy. I just work.

He mentions an impulse to throw away the form which the therapist gave him a few minutes earlier to be filled out by next week. The therapist asks if that is a way of expressing his anger toward him, but P. only says he has a lot of anger, and does not know how much of it is directed toward the therapist. He is angry because he is frustrated "in many areas: personal life, creativity, business." He wishes he could walk up to a woman in the street and "pinch her ass . . . give her behind a little pat. What would happen is, she'd turn around and smile and you'd get into a conversation and probably take her home and make love to her. That's, that's very likely to happen. But the thought is, you know, you can't do that. She'd turn around and slap your face and scream and all that . . . you know, going over and patting some-body on the behind is a little extreme, but you know, I do go over to people sometime and have these little, very shallow bits of interchange and there I've never been rebuffed. . . ."

When asked what he is afraid of, he answers that his "self-image is very inflated . . . and people think I'm someone different than who I really am." He recalls taking excellent care of how he was dressed, and recalls with a laugh how he "would walk around like, er, you know, like I was a real man about town." But now, he is "very consciously trying to dress down." Similarly, he feels the plate on his office door is too "pretentious" for the "little pishika shop" that he has. He was trying to make people think he was "more important than [he] was."

Comment

After being late the previous two sessions, P. comes on time to this one, possibly signaling that his ability to deal with the impending separation from the therapist and therapy has become less fragile. He opens this session by wishing he could pursue his phallic narcissistic heterosexual fantasies. But he cannot, because he does not feel "valid." He blames his wife and other women, almost suggesting a lesbian conspiracy among them. He denies having a sexual interest in his wife's male lover, but recalls a dream in which his *wife* is a lesbian and a bad influence on their daughter. Later in the session, he admits to worries that, as his daughter gets older, she will "see through" him concerning the issue of "why there are no women" in his life. However, he does not connect the two concerns. He recalls attacking his girl friend at age 11 or 12 when she got entangled in a fight he was about to have with a "real faggy kind of mesomorphic lump" of a boy; a few minutes later, he describes himself in very much the same terms as he did that "fruitcake [he] couldn't stand" ("I feel worthless, amorphic, nothingness"). When, later in the session, he agaiń complains of severe insomnia, the therapist brings up P.'s reaction to the impending termination—P. still denies being strongly affected by it, but explores some of the ways in which he was turning off, disengaging from the therapy. P. thus oscillates throughout the session between, on the one hand, omnipotent phallic fantasies and the paranoid, aggressive tendencies, which occur in the wake of their failure and, on the other hand, depressed, deflated, yet calmer and more functional images of himself. However, he does not yet understand these circular dynamics. He does not recognize that, faced with feelings of being abandoned and castrated ("invalid"), he has an impulse to assert himself in phallic, sexual-aggressive exploits with often thinly veiled homosexual feelings; however, he has made progress insofar as he no longer compulsively persists in these fantasies until their ultimate failure results in his breakdown. Instead, he moves into a depressive position in which he is willing to accept himself and function in more realistic terms. Although he does not achieve the insight that would enable him to transcend this "paranoid–depressive" dichotomy, he is now able to oscillate between them with some adaptive ease and functional results, avoiding dangerous extremes and functioning in a more mature way.

SESSION 13

"I was really pissed about the interview with that woman last week. I was startled." (Why?) "You didn't tell me it'd be a woman." P. goes on to report he was hostile to this female psychologist. He didn't like the idea of being questioned by her. Also, he was "very aware of her being a woman, her sexual being . . . it was hot in the room, she played with her skirt and I wanted to tell to her to keep her cunt to herself." He denies being sexually aroused, but then changes his tone to say that he was annoyed and disappointed that he had such a reaction, that he hates women so much. He wonders if his wife is to blame for this, and then recalls almost saying hello to the man he had found in her bed when he saw him in a restaurant the other day. ("I almost said hello to this guy, and I'm supposed to hate him, to want to kill him . . . and I don't have that reaction anymore.") The therapist asks him why he hates women so much, and P. talks of his mother thinking she was doing him a favor when she did things for him, but he feels now it "limited [his] development, sense of responsibility, ability to get out and get things for myself." However, this is more of an intellectual feeling. Still, his first wife had an affair with her boss, and his current wife keeps sending him bills he considers "nonsensical," yet he cannot confront her because he does not want to have an argument with her. "We talk and once in a while it gets genial and I always enjoy that. She and I did have something for a while [and] there's always a little affection that you never get rid of, or wanting affection from that person. . . . What she did to me I consider very dirty and I don't want to have good feelings towards her . . . but it sneaks up once in a while." He returns to talking about the testing with the female psychologist: "She made no overtures, she was professional, but I felt she was [unconsciously] a tease . . . and I was very uncomfortable, I didn't want to do that, I didn't want to make overtures, I didn't want to have her sexually . . . when it came to drawing a woman, I couldn't do it . . . I was really rejecting her . . . except I really . . . I wanted to hold [that] woman in my arms, have a relationship." When the therapist points out this "inconsistency," he replies he "pushes them away" despite their smiles in the street, and exclaims: "It's stuck! It's stuck!" and admits to the "feeling of impotence, not being able to perform." He drifts into a condemnation of present-day dating habits.

Th.: Have you thought some more about the fact that next week is our last session?

Pt.: Uh I thought about it this morning and I was trying. . . . Uh I haven't thought about it consciously, except yesterday, I had to go to my doctor about something and he's a really nice guy and easy to talk to and I mentioned that I was coming here and I, I asked him for stronger sleeping pills. I said I have a lot of anxiety, I still can't, can't sleep and I mentioned that I was coming here and that it was ending in 2 weeks, it was just temporary, so I'm aware of it, but I haven't really reacted. By the way, he gave me, he very hesitantly gave me some barbiturates and he, you know, with a lot of warning that they're highly addictive and not to use' em, at 2 o'clock last night it had no effect on me.

He then mentions problems which make him tense: long-term ("What am I going to do professionally to make a living") and short-term ("loneliness"). He feels too much of a failure to approach a woman:

Well, professionally I'm, I'm no place. Uh you know I'm not, I'm not doing anything exciting. I always use the expression I used to "I want a mountain to climb." I climbed the Matterhorn in Switzerland when I was in Europe. Not all the way to the top, but I, I had to be rescued off the sides, it's kind of a funny story, but you know those kind of intense experiences, er, I haven't had any in years, nothing really dynamic, exciting, er, I feel dull, you know, I probably am cause I'm not turned on and I think if I go out with a woman, you know, a new woman, a new acquaintance, er, I'm not gonna measure up. Which is really silly.

He remarks that he tends to wait for things to come to him—both in business and in relationships. The therapist asks why he thinks he doesn't go out to get more business? P. gives examples of how he did do so rather successfully on isolated occasions.

Th.:   What do you think about, as you said some time ago, being afraid of being a success?
Pt.:   Because I keep rationalizing it's not my style, I prefer small business, I want my free time . . . [but] that's bullshit . . . I'd have to stand up and be counted, be much more demanding with people . . .
Th.:   Be more assertive.
Pt.:   Yeah, which I don't want to be and don't feel able to be . . .

There is a long pause, which ends with the therapist asking P. about the apparent difficulty he reported earlier in completing an evaluation form. He procrastinated, he says, and adds: "the only problem I have with these forms is trying to be really honest and spontaneous with the answers, and I try to please you."

Th.:   Why do you think you want to please me with this form?
Pt.:   Well, I want to please everybody. Uh, I mean you should feel like you've done a good job. Er, I mean, what's crossed my mind several times . . . was writing a book on flatulence, and I think it's realistic, commercial idea . . . it could sell and make a few bucks. I'll never do it. I haven't done anything about it yet, but what crossed my mind is that maybe if I do it in the next year or so, I would send you a copy and just say, you know, I've done it, which would give me a lot of gratification . . .

P. then talks again of his inability to confront people, especially those who are older or authority figures, and mentions some additional problems with that most important client of his. The therapist announces their time is up, and P. says he's going to finish the form the therapist gave him last week, now, "so I don't put it off."

Comment

P. starts by expressing anger at the woman psychologist who tested him the day after the previous session. As usual, he is not immediately able to acknowledge the other side of his ambivalences, that is, that he was attracted to her and "wanted" her. However, he gets there in a roundabout way, by associating to and exploring dynamically equivalent and genetically antecedent conflicts, that is, the tendency to vilify his wife; feelings that his mother prevented him from becoming a real man; positive impulses toward the man who had an affair with his wife. Once he has talked both of hating his wife and still wanting her affection, he can also "discover" that he wanted the female psychologist he was so angry at. He does not understand consciously the road he traveled to become aware of his ambivalence toward the tester, but it is nevertheless a productive trip in which he, more completely than before, uncovers some of his other perennial ambivalences. This awareness, however, makes him feel impotent and depressed. When the therapist now asks for his thoughts about next week's session being their last, he openly relates his anxiety and insomnia to it, as well as considers its impact ("so I'm aware of it, but I haven't really reacted"). This is unlike the previous session, in which he still felt compelled to deny any impact of the pending termination. He goes on to talk of his loneliness, feelings of being dull and professionally unproductive and inept. He explores his "fear of being a success" more fully than heretofore ("I keep rationalizing it's not my style, I prefer small business, I want my free time . . . [but] that's bullshit . . . I'd have to stand up and be counted, be much more demanding with people . . . which I don't want to be and don't feel able to be . . ."). This theme may also be related to P.'s ambivalent acceptance of the therapist's refusal to continue seeing him beyond session 14, which he still feels like challenging but is afraid to do because he "tries to please" the therapist. There is, however, a lot of hostility and defiance in his humble wish to produce and send the therapist a book on, of all things, flatulence. At the end of the session, P. volunteers to remain in the office until he finishes an evaluation form, symbolically expressing his willingness to submit to the therapist's demands if only it will keep the therapist favorably disposed and close.

P. emerges in this session as a more even-keeled, albeit depressed, individual. Instead of verbally indulging in his hate for women, the theme with which he starts the session, he expresses regret and disappointment that this is so. He accepts the therapist's imminent departure from his life, openly talks of the extreme anxiety and depression that it causes him to feel, tries to be mature about it, but cannot help feeling dull and impotent despite the awareness that he can be successful at his work if only he tries.

SESSION 14

"Well, today is the last day," P. opens the session. He thought about it last night and nothing much came to his mind, but there is one thing he's "annoyed" at: he still has "terrible sleeping problems." When asked if he's annoyed at the therapist for not helping him with it, he denies that weakly ("No, not directly, it's mental, but it's also physical"). When asked what might be keeping him awake, he talks of Sunday night being the worst, because the work situation he faces on Monday morning really "bugs" him. Although he always had trouble sleeping, it's been worse these last few months, "roughly since we started." P. evades the therapist's question about what made him sleepless last night, saying it is usually some pressing work problem, but adds that nothing like that "happened for a few weeks and I don't have anything on my mind, but I just can't sleep." The therapist asks if he had any dreams.

Pt.:   I had a couple of peculiar dreams recently . . . One [was] about a lion . . . everybody said you had to fear him, he was a dangerous animal, and it turned out that I just went over to him and petted him and hugged him and there was no danger involved.
Th.:   What do you think of when you think of that dream?
Pt.:   Well, the lion can represent my father, that he wasn't really an ogre and he was really harmless . . .

"Other than that [insomnia?], the week hasn't been too bad," P. continues, and mentions how he thinks a friend of his is really paranoid and "crazy" because he suspects his wife and another women cheated him out of some money. This is the friend with whom P. often identified and with whom he would get together in order to criticize their wives (see sessions 1 and 8). Talking of this reminds P. of his own indecisiveness (e.g., where to go next month for his vacation).

Pt.:   Uh, I'm having a lot of trouble really focusing, I've said this before, and making decisions, and acting, and so on. I'm just all over the place.
Th.:   Tell me as you think about the work we've done over this past period, what do you think you've gained from this program overall?
Pt.:   Uhm, I think I'm a lot calmer than I was. I don't think I'm as highstrung as I was when I came here. The heart attack itself, although I still worry about it, has become much more, much more, much less important. . . . I think things have improved. How much and due to what I'm not sure, but I do feel better generally, there are still some open-ended questions. . . .

The therapist asks what changes would he want to make in his life. It is in his "social and professional life," he says: "Social life, uh, I want it to be much more active, and I'd really like to find one person, a woman that I could hang out with, uh, there's no sign of that happening. The other is to get my business more together. Now, the business is the simpler of the two. You know, it's really easy to do, all I have to do is do it."

When he says that he is not relating to women any better than he did a few months ago, the therapist asks him what he thinks he could do about it? "Well, what everybody tells me to do is to buy a pair of tickets to something, and then walk up to a woman and ask her if she wants to go." But then P. remembers how he excused himself when a friend invited him to his sister's party—"he wanted to fix me up with her." The therapist asks how he thinks he could get over the feelings of fear and hostility toward women? P. doesn't really know, "the thought that comes to my mind is to beat somebody up "like his wife and her mother. I would really like to beat the shit out of her." When asked how this would solve his problems, he responds in a rather confused, rambling, paranoid way about how his wife knows a lot of women in his neighborhood, as if there is some sort of feminist-lesbian conspiracy which might turn against him, and that only reminds him of his own isolation.

Pt.:   I'm isolated, by the way I work and live, I just don't see people. That's probably what I have to do.

Th.:   It's been some time since you talked about your sexual interest in other men. Do you think that's a problem that you still have?

Pt.:   If I was involved with women, uh, that, that thing, it disappears, it comes back when I'm not involved with women. I prefer women, presently.

He feels that the dozen or so women he has slept with is "a miniscule number" compared to other people he has talked with, and he would like to change that. He talks of ideas about joining one of the neighborhood groups but never does. "I guess the fear of meeting . . . new people . . . I have both feelings. I want to with, withdraw also, and not have any contact. But I need contact, I mean I think it's really unhealthy, being a recluse." This leads to his relying on his daughter:

Pt.:   . . . for a lot of things. It's inappropriate . . . and she's having a hard time . . . she's developing normal separation anxiety, you know.

Th.:   Separation from whom?

Pt.:   From me, when she has to go to some place, to her mother's house.

Th.:   How about you. What about you developing a separation anxiety from leaving me?

Pt.:   Not that I felt. One thing I felt is that it's, it's, when I stop coming here, my schedule will be a little less complicated. Between this and the gym and those testing sessions, there's been a lot of daytime interference in my work. I can't concentrate on more than one thing at a time. I really can't. And I used to be able to control a dozen jobs at one time, all in my head. I can't do it. I can only think of one thing at a time. It seems that my brain is becoming less complex.

Th.: Is that good?

Pt.: No, no, I don't think so. I mean the point of relaxing is good. But more than one thing does go on at a time. Particularly if you're running a small business, you have a lot to think about and I'm actually forgetting important things. Forgetting to do them and people call up and I forget what they're talking about, which is no good.

Th.: Do you think that there are things on your mind that interfere with your keeping track of everything you should?

Pt.: I don't feel any conscious things on my mind. I just feel like everything is scrambling and I also feel a little dopey, a little . . . like my mind drifts. I'm not concentrating. I'm not hearing things, things aren't coalescing in my head. They're just drifting around, and some of them are just dribbling in my ears, and I'm, I'm not the same as I was.

Th.: When?

Pt.: I think before the heart attack. But even after the heart attack when I went back to work, which I did too soon, I went right back to work, er I tried to remain cool and then I started getting hyper again by getting super-involved in work. And than I put a stop to it. Since I put a stop to it, it's been downhill.

He has been "screwing things up, made a lot of mistakes in the last month or two." which cost him money. He talks of feeling over-whelmed by all the domestic work and looking after his daughter. It would be easier if he had a baby-sitter, "a regular mother's helper," but he doesn't because he does not feel he can afford it. He mentions that his daughter prefers to be with him, anyway, and then says how she is:

Pt.: . . . gonna grow up eventually and leave me.

Th.: Well, how do you feel about that idea?

Pt.: That disturbs me a great deal.

Th.: Why?

Pt.: Wh, because then I'll be completely alone.

When the therapist "reminds" P. that his wife left him, his daughter will leave him, and he is leaving him today, he replies, "c'est la vie," but adds that what disturbs him most now is that he feels "wishy-washy," he doesn't feel any strong feelings, any drive, even his anxiety is "kind of amorphic and dull." He talks of financial worries, and possible insecurity in the future. He is worried about getting sick, the possibility of another heart attack. Then he says:

Pt.: Like right now, I feel like I'm getting senile. I feel like my brain is going to sleep. I need an electric shock therapy or something, some electric,

electric shock up my ass, that's what I need. Cause I'm really . . . energizing, enervation. I just, like that, drained of all my intellectual energy, psychic energy. I need something really exciting.

Th.:   What, what do you consider exciting?

Pt.:   Oh, I would love to produce a play or climb a mountain or do a colossal piece of art work or have a, you know, 48-hour sexual marathon with my sister-in-law.

Then, as P. mentions some concrete steps he will take come September, the therapist sounds a supportive note:

Th.:   You sound as though you're functioning. Things are going along; you don't seem terribly upset about anything.

Pt.:   No, I'm not, I'm functioning, I mean my daughter and I do things, not enough according to her, but we eat and I go to work. Uh, it just all seems so mediocre.

P. talks some more of his sleeplessness. The therapist asks if there is anything he would like to tell him before they stop?

Pt.:   I've been thinking about whether I should continue any kind of therapy or not. I don't feel like I really need any kind of therapy. I did a while ago, I was really panicky. I don't feel that panic anymore. I'm, I don't know what else I could do with a therapist. I feel that . . . I, which I thought before, after I stopped going to Dr. X., the rest is up to me, I just gotta shit or get off the pot and nobody can do that for me. That's it.

Th.:   Okay, good luck.

Pt.:   Thank you very much.

Th.:   Goodbye.

Pt.:   Thank you for the 3 months.

Th.:   Righto.

Comment

P., for the first time, opens the session by a comment on the dominant transference issue ("Well, today is the last day"). However, he still appears to be feeling unable to deal with it fully, as is evident from his immediate detour into talking about his sleeping difficulties, which he could not resist tracing to the beginning of the therapy (even though the insomnia was a problem he similarly complained of in session 1). Still, P. does not mount a direct or indirect attack on the therapist aimed at inducing him to continue the therapy. It is in this context of being able to deal with the therapist's imminent departure without resorting to his more primitive defenses that P. is able to have his lion dream and self-interpret it as meaning that his father "wasn't really an ogre and was really harmless." But, just as P.'s dream unrealistically portrays the lion as harmless, so too, P.'s feeling about himself and the therapy are similarly unrealistically portrayed as impotent and weak. He is able to express warm feelings and appreciation for the therapist, as well as for what he accomplished in the therapy, but this is accompanied by feelings that he does not need any kind of therapy and that he and his life are doomed to be dull and empty ("I'm functioning, my daughter and I do things, not enough according to her, but we eat and I go to work"). These feelings of castration and abandonment invariably lead to manifestly denied but clearly prominent homosexual masochistic urges ("some electric shock up my ass, that's what I need") and omnipotent phallic aggressive fantasies ("to produce a play, or climb a mountain or do a colossal piece of art work or . . . have a 48-hour sexual marathon with my sister-in-law"). Still, rather than being acted out to their bitter end, these impulses and fantasies remain in the background, as P. demonstrates his increased tolerance toward and awareness of his ambivalences, vulnerabilities, and imperfections. The price he pays is increased resignation and some quiet sadness, but there is no more self-destructive rage and acting out as was seen in sessions 8, 9, and 10, and throughout much of his life history. His basic character has not changed and the underlying core conflicts are hardly changed, but he is more aware of them and a shift has occurred, which makes him better adapted and more realistic.

6

Converging Data: The Psychological Testings

THE FIRST TEST BATTERY

The patient was given a complete battery of psychological tests at the start of his 14 weeks of brief psychotherapy, a retest near the completion of the therapy (about 2½ months later), and a third battery about 8 months following the termination of therapy. The first battery was administered by a male graduate student in psychology under the supervision of Dr. S., and the second and third batteries were administered by Dr. S. The batteries were all done blind with respect to what was taking place in the treatment.

For the initial testing, the patient was given the Rorschach, TAT, WAIS, Figure Drawings, Bender Gestalt, and a writing sample test. The two retests consisted of the Rorschach, TAT, Figure Drawing, and the writing sample.

On the first battery, P. obtained a full scale WAIS IQ of 136 (Verbal IQ = 132; Performance IQ = 135). This placed him in the "Very Superior" category of intellectual functioning. One of the most striking aspects of P.'s projective responses on the first protocol was the preponderance of poorly controlled hostile and sexual feelings. This, in conjunction with a lack of evidence on the projective tests of benign relationships, suggested that the patient experienced himself as alone in a hostile and condemning world, a victim of his own desperate impulses. He is without a containing figure, someone to absorb violent feelings and to help him neutralize them.

The images tended to fuse sexual and aggressive themes: Card IV—

"A fat grotesque woman . . . she is devouring a figure that is standing between her legs and she has already devoured the head of the figure through her vagina." Card V—"looks a little bit like a vagina with a very erect clitoris and of course it has grippers on the bottom." The primitive rage, which so often overwhelms P., is often related, as the previous images suggest, to feeling extremely threatened by women, whom he perceives as being aggressive and hurtful. The first battery depicted women, for the most part, as dangerous and devouring; as possessors of mysterious powers that they wield over the masculine world. Envy of women is also evident in images where women are portrayed as sexually potent and powerful and men are depicted as sexually impotent and inadequate. Images of castration and hermaphroditism, and images expressing concerns with homosexuality also occur frequently in the Rorschach. For example, on Card III, he sees "two African women with erections, doing something to a man's gonads, there's blood all around and they're trying to steal's the man's masculinity; an effeminant penis with no testicles; and two men reaching out to touch each other, it's pleasurable but they're standing back at the same time." Similarly, on the TAT, there are stories in which he fuses sexuality and aggression and reveals his homosexual concerns. In response to Card 13MF, he says, "A man with an erection has murdered a woman, he possibly really enjoyed murdering her as a sexual thing." In response to Card 4, he says, "A man has told a woman that he's homosexual, and he's feeling dejected and embarrassed." In response to Card 8BM, he says, "A boy who is homosexual has shot his father because he has strong homosexual feelings toward his father."

The projectives on the first battery also abound in deteriorating and damaged images, suggesting that the patient feels damaged, wounded, in danger of being harmed, and has a self-image that is negative and distorted. This sense of inadequacy about himself stands in contrast to his tendency to overidealize others and then to despair because of his inability to live up to the ideals he has created. Some of the images expressing his low self-esteem and a sense of damage are: "A ram's scull . . . the way a skeleton looks after cartilage has rotted away" (Card IV); "a winged figure . . . very small for size of figure which is gross—big and heavy—small head—small wings—but very fat gross body and very tiny feet" (Card IV); " a monster with floppy hands . . . very fat, rolling fat and uglified" (Card IV); "an Adam's apple . . . broken in the center—there is a piece missing" (Card VIII); "seahorse-type animals, looking at each other and snickering . . . long misshapen noses and pinheads" (Card IX).

A salient theme that appeared in the projective tests was one of being a disappointment to authority figures as well as a fear of them being harsh and disapproving. His tendency to overidealize others at the expense of his own feelings of worth are best expressed in some of the TAT stories: 7BM—"Father and son—the son is a kind of failure and father a lot more worldly—he has more experience and confidence—just went through experience where son is feeling dejected—father telling him it's alright and not so serious—but son knows father is wrong and it is hopeless—son can't possibly live up to what the father expects;" 6BM—"mother is facing terrible financial stress and the son is unable to help in any way—she feels he hasn't lived up to her expectations and he feels the same way—like a complete failure," and, this "mother just caught the same little boy masturbating—terribly embarrassed—mother stupid about it and he's forever hung up" (Card 5).

Stories of object loss and subsequent despair, depression, and suicide were common on the first TAT, reflecting the other side of his feelings toward the rejecting parents, that is, a longing for love and acceptance. In response to Card 15, he says: "This guy is suffering pain at the loss of not one person—the loss of a lot of people or of life—feeling like he lost a lot of things—which in reality he has and possibly trying to dive down into the space where those things are—he wants to recapture his life which has slipped away—outcome is that he'll walk away and nothing will be changed." In response to Card 14, he gives the following story: "This guy is about to jump out the window and take his life because he just feels that life isn't worth it—but I think he feels all of a sudden while looking out the window that it's dawn and is a start of a new day and springtime and maybe it's not so bad after all. He doesn't jump out the window—he struggles on." In another story (3BM) he says: "Woman who just feels complete dejection and has contemplated suicide—is a scissor lying on the floor? But she couldn't go through with it—her life is totally fucked up—nobody loves her and she is doomed to live like that for the rest of her life."

The extent of the patient's unmodulated primitive feelings, difficulty integrating affect and ideation, wide use of splitting as a defense, and extremely poor self-regard resulted in lapses in reality testing and disordered thought functioning in the first test battery. His F + % was 54% and his extended F + % was 75%. He had three confabulatory responses, four confabulatory tendencies, nine fabulized combinations, and nine fabulized and two peculiar verbalizations. The lapses in thinking and reality testing occurred most frequently in relation to his feelings of anxiety and around women, and his difficulty modulating primitive feelings involving sex and aggression. However, P. did exhibit strengths and adaptive qualities that prevented these tendencies from manifesting as more serious pathology. He is often aware when his thinking is primarily on a fantasy level, and he is able to recover from these fantasies. There is a looseness and fluidity to this thinking, which allows him to shift from more primary process and affectively-oriented levels of thinking to more reality-oriented levels without evidence of irreversible regression or decompensation. The evidence from the first test battery led to a diagnosis of Borderline Personality Disorder with marked Depressive Features.

THE SECOND TEST BATTERY

The second testing, administered about 12 to 13 weeks after the first, showed much improved modulation of aggression and violent sexual feelings as well as an increased capacity to neutralize, with more positive affect, some of his overwhelming destructive feelings. There was also less thought disorder and disorganization. There was more of a craving for warmth, lovingness, and approval on this testing as opposed to the first battery, which was dominated by images of dangerous and devouring women. As the dominant themes shifted from perceptions of parental figures being harsh and punitive to being more warm, affectionate, and sensitive, the patient, in feeling more longing, also experienced an increase in anxiety and vulnerability. A greater ability to integrate good and bad feelings, less of a sense of being damaged, improvement in reality testing, and less of a tendency to regress into fantasy are all more evident on the second battery. Along with these positive changes, there were less human responses, a tendency to use denial more frequently as a defense, and to adopt a pollyannish stance as well as a more felt experience of impotence and helplessness as a result of giving up some of his powerful all good or all bad imagos.

Many dramatic changes were evident from comparing scores on the structural summary sheet. The F + % went from 54% to 82% and the extended F + % from 75% to 86%, indicating a marked improvement in reality testing. The F% went from 46% to 50%, and the extended F% went from 86% to 100%, suggesting a greater ability to modulate affect and to integrate affect and ideation. The EB ratio went from M10:C4.5 to M3.5:C3. This represents a shift to a better balance between affect and fantasy ideation, and less of a tendency to withdraw into fantasy life. There was also a significant decrease in thought disorder. On the retest, there were 11 fabulized responses, 3 fabulized combinations, and 1 confabulized response. He went from one FC on the first test to 6 FCs on the second test, indicating an increased capacity to gain control over his emotions and not feel overwhelmed. There was a decrease in the percentage of human responses—from 42% on the first battery to 27% on the second. This may be explained by the fact that the patient may have had to distance himself somewhat from experiences with other people in order to gain more control over his feelings and to feel less disorganized.

The figure drawings on the second test were drawn with softer lines, were less rigid, and exhibited less turmoil. His second house was less decorated, had no chimney, and was drawn from a front view as opposed to the side view of the first house. This suggested that in the second drawing the patient was less defended, exhibiting less of a macho front, and was perhaps less paranoid. The second house also allowed for easier access.

There were several responses on the projectives in the second battery that reflect the budding awareness of new, previously unacknowledged feelings. Along with this, a tremendous fear and anxiety is experienced in regard to these unfamiliar feelings. On Card IX of the Rorschach, he says, "A union is being produced, seed of the unknown—which might be malevolent. . . . When whole thing looks so happy and something is unknown could be dangerous . . . something coming to put a damper on whole thing." And on Card 7BM of the TAT, he says:

> These are two brothers. One's much older than the other. Not brothers—it's father and son. I'd rather it be brothers but it's not. The father has just said something much softer and more sensitive than he usually does. Son is disturbed because it interferes with image of his father. The father has just expressed some affection which he never did before and the son feels very angry about it. He wants to dislike father. Father usually doesn't treat him well. This little crack in ice is disturbing because it doesn't fit in. The son is about to leave. After he leaves the father dies, which makes the son even angrier.

This story is in marked contrast to the first story to the same card where the father is seen as rejecting and the son feels a sense of hopelessness about living up to the father's high expectations.

Whereas the first battery was flooded with images of woman as dangerous and devouring, the second battery reveals images reflecting a craving for warmth and a concern with his own impotence. Card IV on the first Rorschach elicited images of "rotting skeletons," "monsters with rolling fat and uglified," and, "grotesque woman who devours the heads of figures with her vagina." The second battery elicited this response on Card IV:

> This gives me a warm feeling. Similar to work of artist in Leonard Baskin.

Looks like archangel—Benevolent angel. Has ugly distorted body—but not the kind that is repulsive. Has wings that are too small for body which means it's impotent—can't harm you, doesn't have much poison. Looks like it could wrap arms around you—be warm and loving. Fact that wings are small made it not threatening. Had very fat legs—fat ripples on surface like a very fat woman. [ripples?] Actual *texture* on the edge of the drawing.

On Card V of the first battery, he saw "a human figure coming at you about to clutch you in huge arms or wings like a female figure— probably smother you—females are the kind that do the smothering." On the second Rorschach to the same card, he says, "Insect flying away from viewer. . . . Harmed insect with tail . . . beating down with wings . . . having a hard time getting off ground. Doesn't want viewer to see front of body. . . . Trying very hard to run away. . . . Looks like ends of wings are wet—can't get going." Here, he is clearly experiencing more of his vulnerability and helplessness, his own impotence, rather than feeling victimized, and pursued by the smothering female.

Originally, on Card VI, he saw a vagina with grippers and a very effeminate penis, decorated with feathers, in two different responses. On the retest, he saw a hermaphrodite with both sexual symbols: "Has decorated penis . . . underneath is female sexual organ sort of like vagina is supporting penis. Without vagina, penis would fall and crumble—would not be able to hold itself erect." There is an attempt in the second testing to integrate these previously split images in a way that might lead to some harmony rather than destruction.

There are also indications on the second battery that his feelings of being damaged and destroyed are lessening. Whereas on the first test he sees a voice box on Card VIII: "broken in the center with a piece missing," on the retest he sees: "a larynx that looks light and airy—the kind that would produce sweet tones—not heavy."

On the second TAT, there are indications that he perceives parental figures and authorities as less harsh, punitive, and critical. On Card 5 of the retest, he says:

> The mother came in and found the boy masturbating. She doesn't seem as shocked as she did last time I saw picture. Last time, she looked very surprised. It almost looks like she's looking in on kid to see if he's okay. Whatever he's doing. She is going to very quietly shut the door and walk away. She doesn't have much feelings about it. . . ."

There is also more evidence on the second test of his ability to integrate polarized feelings—to hold them in awareness at the same time and to experience ambivalence rather than just one extreme or the other. On Card 14 of the second TAT, he says:

This man has mixed feelings. He's looking out at a new day, but he is also contemplating jumping out the windows. He doesn't jump. He just hangs on continually. It's very obviously a positive/negative illustration. Way it's drawn, goes back and forth between positive and negative drawing. Before you look at subject matter, you feel this ambivalence. You can look at either all the blackness or whiteness coming through.

The depression and feeling of loss is much less acute on the retest and there are no indications of suicidal ideation. One can speculate that some of the changes may be related to the therapist fostering in P. more involvement with his inner life and allowing him to feel safer in voicing his concerns. He thus feels less suspicious and in danger from threatening figures.

FOLLOW-UP TESTING: THE THIRD TEST BATTERY

The third battery, however, showed that these bad introjects have not been done away with. Administered 8 months after the second, this battery showed evidence of increased paranoia, a sense that the patient had become more fearful of external dangers, and more openly despairing and depressed. Balancing this was evidence that many of the formal changes evident on the second battery were preserved, as well as some of the openness and vulnerability. Reality testing remained intact (F + % = 75%–88%). The improved balance in the EB ratio was also maintained (EB 3:3). There is a continuation of a decrease in CF scores (indicating less impulsiveness) and a continuation of the increase in FCh (anxiety experienced). There is a return, in the third battery, to some of the violent feelings toward women, fear of violence from women, and images suggesting a reemergence of a poor self-image and self-destructive feelings. This was illustrated with images on the Rorschach like "a bat, probably beating itself to death, devilish, clownish faces, concealed in their torsos . . . each have evil part not to be trusted" and "a big leaf that's starting to wither and die." These images suggest not so much a concern with parental figures being harsh and disapproving as in the first battery, but an experience of them being negligent, unprotective, and, perhaps, indifferent to his agony.

The denial and pollyannaish defenses which became apparent in the second battery were less prominent in the third battery. The patient seemed to experience his aggression, sexual impulses, despair, and suicidal feelings more immediately, and seemed to be less defended against the expression of them. Card 1 of the Rorschach starts out directly with "hooded female figure about to grab someone and strangle them" and his second response is a "fox's face—kind of meaningless." This is in contrast to the second battery where he saw a "pelvis" first and then "a friendly fox," both responses reflecting more defensiveness and denial.

The weakening in defenses is accompanied by a slight increase in thought disorder, suggesting that there may be some lowering in the patient's boundaries from the time of second battery. There is also a marked decrease in pure F responses, indicating a possible increase in the patient's access to his fantasy and emotional life. An increased articulation of suicidal feelings and despair was also evident in the third battery. These changes would support the view that the patient's boundaries have weakened.

There were also several images and verbalizations on the Rorschach that suggested the patient had become increasingly paranoid and fearful of external dangers. On Card VII, he sees two women who are "nice and seductive—each have evil part, not to be trusted" and on Card VIII, he says, "I feel this card is very sneaky because it's done in happy colors. We all know it's not true. It's meant to deceive. It's probably made out of stinking shit." Similarly, on TAT Card 15 he says, "This is another fake drawing, playing and showing nonsense. Nobody cares who dies. This drawing pokes fun. The figure is supposed to look like he's sad but he is not, he's play acting. He's almost smacking his hands together in relish." With the inner boundaries weakening and the patient being more directly in contact with frightening feelings of rage and despair, he seems to be externalizing and projecting some of these inner dangers and experiencing himself being threatened from the outside as well as the inside.

Although there is an increased expression of despairing and suicidal thoughts in the content of responses both on the Rorschach and TAT, this is not paralleled with similar changes in the formal qualities (i.e., there is not more color shading, shading, more black and white color, marked decrease in human responses or diminished reality testing). This suggests a firmer defense organization than was seen in the first battery, but one that is not as inflexible as the organization that was present in the second battery. He is better able to tolerate this degree of depressing anxiety without formal regression.

The TAT also reflected more direct open anger, particularly at women and mother figures, as on Card 5 where he says, with less compliance, "This is same as it was last time. Mother just walked in and found boy masturbating. Boy knows he's been discovered. From then on for the rest of his life he'll be ashamed of himself. He'll never get rid of it. She is a real bitch." There is more open defiance, as on

Card I: "This kid is very disgusted. Mother wants him to play violin. He's a genius at playing it—a prodigy. But he hates playing it. In about 5 minutes, he'll smash it to smithereens and that will be absolute end—picture won't exist anymore." The stories suggest he is no longer pursuing his mother or her representative and he is trying more effectively to separate from her. On Card 6BM, he says, "This is man and mother again. They've come to blows. Everything is out in the open. He's hurt her and she's hurt him and after this, they part company. He feels terrible, very angry and embarrassed. She feels sad but she'll go on playing cards and having a good time." But his less guarded rage belies the fact that the desire for such concern and protectiveness is not far under the surface. In fact, on TAT Card 7BM, he hopes to reencounter "the ghost of his father . . . and the man is thinking of seeing his father again when he dies. He knows under those circumstances, the father will be much kinder and more benevolent than he was in real life."

There was also evidence throughout the testing of increased reflective awareness, as on TAT Card 13MF ("feel like I'm being over-dramatic") and TAT Card 4 ("He knows it's ridiculous"). On the figure drawings, he put more emphasis on the faces of the figures and the top of the body. The features of the face were clearer and the drawings less stylized. The man and woman both had a more open stance than in previous drawings. The house was also more open, with many windows, situated in an airy, beach-like surrounding. For the tree, he drew mainly the trunk, with very little of the roots and branches showing. It suggested he was very preoccupied with his "self" in the present, which he was able to experience more clearly, but that he was cut off from the past and future, and perhaps feeling somewhat alienated and alone.

In summary, it appears that the patient has maintained the internalized image of the "benign therapist" and many of the formal changes that were evident in the second battery. These changes seem directly attributable to the results of treatment. However, without the therapist's continued presence, the patient appears to have experienced increased stress and difficulty managing the inner world of feelings to which he was opened up. The more open despair, direct expression of rage, and decreased defensiveness and denial apparent on the third battery (appearing at first to be a regressive trend), may in fact indicate that the patient, because of the internalization of the benign aspects of the therapist, allowed himself to be more open to previously forbidden aspects of himself. The increase in anxious and depressive content without a decrease in the level of formal functioning suggests some improvement in the patient's ability to tolerate anxiety and depression. It seems that the changes that came about as a result of treatment became integrated sufficiently so that he cannot return to his former self, but he is still not at ease in experiencing much of his previously denied self. Without the continued support of the therapist, he is still quite terrified of these warded off aspects of self experience.

TRANSFERENCE MANIFESTATIONS IN THE PSYCHOLOGICAL TESTINGS

The first test battery was administered after the first of 14 weekly psychotherapy sessions, before a relationship had developed in treatment. As was noted above, the test responses reflected a preponderance of poorly controlled hostile and sexual feelings. This, in conjunction with lack of evidence on the tests of benign relationships, suggests that the patient experienced himself as quite alone in a hostile and condemning world, a victim of his own desperate impulses. He was without a containing figure, someone to absorb these violent feelings and to help him neutralize them.

A dominant theme that came up with regard to father, mother, and other authority figures was one of being a disappointment to them. There was, as well, the fear of them being harsh and disapproving. This was most clearly seen on two TAT stories where he responded with the "son can't possibly live up to what the father expects," and, about the mother, he says, "she feels he [the son] hasn't lived up to her expectations and he feels the same way—like a complete failure." These feelings were also expressed in the initial phases of therapy. P. talked of his father's inability to express affection and his cold, critical, rejecting attitude toward him. But there were also feelings of sadness, loss, and anger expressed toward the father who died 15 years ago. Themes of object loss, despair, depression, and even suicidal ideation were abundant on the psychological tests, reflecting the other side of his feelings toward the rejecting parents—a longing for love and acceptance. On Card 3BM, he says of the woman in the card, "nobody loves her and she is doomed to live like that for the rest of her life."

In the first battery, women were, for the most part, described as threatening, dangerous, and devouring. Images of castration and hermaphroditism ("two women with erections") were frequent, as were themes of homosexuality. These all imply (among other things) that women are perceived as dangerously powerful and that he has a need to flee from them—perhaps toward homosexual relationships. Although in the early part of the treatment the patient described his mother as a wonderful and loving person, he soon talked about negative feelings toward her as a response to unrealistic expectations of him. As his trust in the therapist increased, he talked more freely of his anger toward his wife and other women who he viewed as castrating and hurtful to him.

The second psychological test battery, which was administered 14 weeks later at the end of treatment, showed much improved modulation of aggression and violent sexual feelings as well as an increased capacity to neutralize, with more positive affect, some of these overwhelming destructive feelings. This strongly suggests that the patient was not only able to develop and sustain a positive transference toward the therapist, but he was able to internalize more benign aspects and attitudes of the therapist to help himself deal with the malevolent parental imagos that were evoking so much self-hatred, violence, and conflict in his internal world. This marked shift, particularly in his attitude toward father figures, is most evident in his statement on TAT Card 7BM in the second battery: "He wants to dislike father. Father usually doesn't treat him well. This little crack in ice is disturbing because it doesn't fit in."

Whereas the first battery shows, predominantly, themes and images reflecting the patient's experience of woman as castrating, dangerous, and devouring, there is evidence in the second battery of an increase in the craving for warmth. As the dominant transference themes shift from the perception of parental figures being harsh and punitive to being more warm, affectionate, and sensitive, the patient, in feeling more longing, also experiences an increase in anxiety and vulnerability.

The relationship with the therapist has fostered more involvement with his inner life and allowed him to feel safer in voicing his concerns. He thus feels less paranoid and in danger from threatening figures. In the latter part of therapy, the therapist also noted that the patient was less grandiose and paranoid (which paralleled findings in the testing) and more depressed (which did not parallel findings in the testing). On the second test, there were, in fact, diminished themes of loss and depression and less suicidal ideation.

The third psychological test battery revealed an increase in paranoid ideation, a sense that the patient had once more become fearful of external dangers, and more open despair and depression, all suggesting that, to some extent, he had lost the sense of the presence of a protective, containing therapist. Balancing this, there was evidence that many of the structural changes evident on the second battery were preserved, and that he still retained some of the openness and vulnerability that was present there. In the absence of the therapist who helped him neutralize some of his destructive feelings, we witness here a return of some of the violent feelings toward women, as well as the fear of violence from women. There is also a reemergence of images suggestive of a poor self-image and self-destructive feelings. This was illustrated with images on the Rorschach like "a bat, probably beating itself to death, devilish, clownish faces, concealed in their torsos . . . each have evil part not to be trusted" and "a big leaf that's starting to wither and die." These images suggest not so much a concern with parental figures being harsh and disapproving, as in the first battery, but rather an experience of them being negligent, unprotective, and perhaps indifferent to his agony. But his less-guarded rage belies the fact that the desire for such concern and protectiveness is not far under the surface. In fact, on TAT Card 7BM, he hopes to reencounter "the ghost of his father. . . . and the man is thinking of seeing his father again when he dies. He knows under those circumstances, the father will be much kinder and benevolent than he was in real life." So the benign father–therapist is not forgotten, nor are the benefits of the relationship lost, but in the absence of the actual containing, protective relationship, the more violent, destructive, and paranoid fears return and his transference images become again more threatening.

STRUCTURAL REORGANIZATION IN THE PSYCHOLOGICAL TEST RESPONSES

The brief interval between the first and second battery (3 months) is considered by some to be an insufficient amount of time to reflect true change in personality structure. Harrower (1958), for example, detected either no improvement or weak improvement on projective tests given at termination in an extensive test–retest study of change in relatively short-term psychotherapy. She found much greater changes subsequent to long-term psychotherapy and concluded that "time is necessary for changes to become sufficiently a part of the personality so that they register through the medium of the test material" (p. 265). However, the findings in the current test–retest study varied from those of Harrower in that we did find changes on the second and third retest batteries that correspond to Schafer's (1967) "relatively reliable indices of structural change" and to his definition of change of structure. Schafer (1979) suggests that:

. . . change includes lasting modification of preferred defensive measures, the direction being from more to less archaic and ego-limiting defense; more command on the ego's part over modes of activity previously dominated by id and superego trends; decreased inter- and intra-systemic conflict; improved efficiency of such ego functions as reality testing and synthesis; the attainment of stable and gratifying relations with others; also, increased reserves of neutralized energy and improved capacity for neutralizing the energies of the id and superego, as manifest in reduced regression rate and decreased power of infantile instinctual fixations. Reference might also be made to maturer forms of narcissism and the completion of separation-individuation and the attainment of object constancy (p. 887).

Schafer also sees genuine character change as coming about in the analytic situation when the analysand is:

living in vastly more complex worlds with vastly more complex repertoires of action, including the actions of representations of self and others in relation. They give different accounts of their lives and prospects. They believe in nonincestuous sexuality, in vaginas that are neither cloacal nor containers of teeth or hidden penises, in love that is not devouring, etc. (p. 886).

Additionally, he states that:

all change of content is redescribable as change of structure and vice versa. . . . For example when a fantasy of exalted power replaces a fantasy of utter helplessness, one is observing a change of content with little gain in adaptiveness and long range stability; . . . in contrast, when an analysand steadily maintains and implements ideals of realistic appraisal of what he or she can and will do reliably, when earlier that analysand communicated only fantasies of helplessness or of grandiose power or swings between the two, one is observing a change of content with considerable and observable adaptive consequences. (pp. 888–889)

Schafer (1967) cautions skepticism of more superficial changes that may be the result of transference cures or resistance maneuvers. Although much of what we found in our second and third retest batteries could be a function of the shifting transference manifestations, there was also a significant amount of change which is consistent with what Schafer considers to be structural: (a) a decrease in thought disorder; (b) an increase in the capacity to respond with affect and to modulate it appropriately; (c) an increased ability to perceive human images; and (d) an overall degree of perceptual accuracy of response. In addition, the patient exhibited, on the second battery; (a) improved modulation of aggression and of violent sexual feelings as well as an increased capacity to neutralize, with more positive affect, some of his over-whelming destructive feelings; (b) improved ability to integrate good and bad feelings; (c) less of a sense of being damaged; (d) improved reality testing; and (e) less of a tendency to regress into fantasy.

We also saw a shift in perception from parental figures being harsh and punitive to being warmer, more affectionate, and sensitive; and women being less devouring and dangerous. Such a change in perception of others allowed the patient to feel more longing and vulnerability. This difference in the two batteries is in line with Schafer's idea that genuine change would involve the patient developing a more complex repertoire of action, including the actions of representations of self and other in relation. In shifting from an experience of love that is devouring and/or incestuous to one that is warmer and less feared, there is a clear alteration in self-perception as well as perception of others.

There were also indications of change of content in fantasy that would suggest change in structure. Essentially, the extremes of his powerful all good or all bad images give way in the second battery to more integrated images, suggesting more realistic appraisal of others and himself, leading to more adaptive consequences. Father figures are not as rejecting and women not as dangerous and devouring; stories are told of people with mixed feelings and feelings of ambivalence.

In line with this latter finding, we saw increased signs of anxiety and vulnerability as testing progressed, which seem to be due to the patient's increased openness to more appropriate object relations. Schwager and Spear (1981), in examining the test–retest protocols of 10 schizophrenic patients, found that change in these patients was often marked by increased disorganization, thought disorder, and regression. This was understood as improvement, in that the patient was able to loosen himself from a rigid, often paranoid defensive structure, and allow himself greater access to unconscious, conflictual impulses because of an increased capacity for integration and appropriate object relations. Similarly, the increased anxiety and vulnerability here was thought to represent a shift toward greater cognitive and interpersonal flexibility, which could lead to the expansion and integration of the patient's personality, and thus to psychological improvement.

The most significant changes in the second battery seem to be related to the patient's positive transference and to his internalizing and identifying with benign aspects and attitudes of the therapist. The latter increased his ability to deal with the malevolent parental images, which were evoking so much self-hatred, violence, and conflict in his internal world. The relationship with the therapist fostered more involvement with his inner life, and allowed him to feel safer in voicing his concerns. He thus exhibited less paranoid ideation in the test material. In the latter part of therapy, the therapist had also noted that the patient was less grandiose and paranoid in sessions, paralleling findings in the testing.

The patient's responses to the third battery maintained many of the formal changes evident in the second battery. In addition, there was also evidence of increased regression and a reemergence of the patient's bad introjects. This suggests a weakening of the partially internalized identification with the protective, containing therapist. In the absence of the therapist, who helped him neutralize some of his destructive feelings, there is a return to images of being destroyed, devoured, untrusting, and unprotected.

The patient's behavior during the third testing session also indicated a wish on his part to be united with the benevolent father (therapist). He articulated suicidal feelings and said specifically that he had the fantasy of cutting his wrists in the testing session. His verbalizations made it necessary for Dr. S. to contact his former therapist so that he could assess the real danger in this situation. The patient was thus successful in inducing the tester to reunite him with the "benevolent father." But, as was noted previously, the increase of suicidal and despairing thoughts were not paralleled by similar changes in the formal qualities, and this suggests that the patient was better able to tolerate depression and anxiety without formal regression.

Thus the third battery shows that much of the positive experience with the therapist is retained and many of the changes that resulted from the internalization of the therapist as a benign figure are evident, even after 8 months without treatment. Yet, the increased regression, expression of despair, and paranoid ideation suggest that the patient is unable to sustain this higher level of functioning without the continued presence of the therapist as a reality in his life.

Many of the changes observed in this case are in line with what the literature has defined as "real change." However, questions should be raised about whether 14 weeks of therapy were enough to bring about permanent structural reorganization. One possibility for understanding the rather dramatic changes that appeared in the patient's test behavior would be to view these changes in terms of the patient's previous level of functioning. Thus, through development of a positive transference, the patient was able to raise his level of functioning to a higher preexisting one. In this light, the changes observed here would be the result of providing treatment conditions which allowed a more optimal level of previous functioning to emerge.

Although, the patient's level of stress decreased and his level of functioning increased during the period he was in treatment, the termination seemed to come too abruptly for him; althought leaving with some benefit, the patient experienced an increase of anxiety and depression at the end, suggesting that it might have been beneficial to continue treatment for a longer period of time. Although the results of this single case cannot be generalized to all short-term therapies, they do suggest the need for more careful scrutiny of follow-up data in those treatment cases for which short-term therapists claim "complete success."

7

Technical Neutrality and Therapeutic Focus in Brief Psychotherapy

It was our purpose, in the present monograph, to demonstrate the occurrence, in a brief psychoanalytic psychotherapy, of processes characteristic of long-term classical psychoanalytic treatment. Specifically, we were interested in developing conviction that a short-term treatment, conducted along appropriate psychoanalytic lines, could reveal a central process characteristic of the classical psychoanalytic approach. Thus we wished to demonstrate that transference, as it is generally understood, would emerge and rapidly coalesce into a transference paradigm, provided that our treatment approach did not attempt to actively manipulate the patient–therapist relationship in a predetermined way. Our sense of the present case, from both our process summaries and our converging psychological test batteries, encourages our conviction that the present form of short-term psychoanalytic psychotherapy does demonstrate the development of a natural transference paradigm, and suggests to us that this form of psychotherapy could be usefully pursued for the study of process variables characteristic of classical psychoanalytic treatment.

Our discussion of the conduct of this case will focus on two aspects of the treatment that we feel played a powerful role in the development, intensification, and subsequent partial working through of the transference paradigm identified here. These aspects are the technical neutrality of the therapist, and our view of therapeutic focus and its relevance to the transference paradigm that emerged.

TECHNICAL NEUTRALITY

Before considering the technical neutrality of the therapeutic stance utilized in the treatment of our patient, we wish to highlight a distinction recently made clear by Lipton (1977) between the therapist's technical behavior (i.e., analyzing behavior vis-à-vis the patient), and his personal or idiosyncratic characteristics, which define him as different from other therapists. What we are concerned with here is the technical approach to this patient rather than the unique characteristics of this particular therapist, although recognizing that such characteristics do affect the transference. Indeed, it was clear from the patient's immediate reactions to the therapist that his age, style, and appearance were crucial aspects of the patient's positive transference reactions early in treatment. While not discounting the effects of such characteristics, we are more interested here in the analyst's technical management of the transference wishes than of elements intrinsic to the analyst's character or style.

We also wish to distinguish the stance of technical neutrality from the context of the treatment situation itself. In this brief psychotherapy, the context of the treatment differed from the classical context in several respects. The imposition of time-limits, taping of the sessions, the upright face-to-face position, the absence of fee, and the frequency of visits all affected the treatment context in significant ways. Despite these alterations of the classical analytic situation, the therapeutic stance toward the patient remained, for the most part, neutral. From our perspective, it is this neutral stance which we feel to be the essential technical element that is necessary for the development of an analytic process (Brenner, 1976), and it does seem that the emergence of a transference paradigm in the present case supports this view. It is, therefore, the uniquely analytic attitude established by the therapist that allows the core conflicted prototypic relationship theme to emerge. This analytic attitude enables those elements that are intrinsic to the prototypic relationship conflicts to coalesce into a transference paradigm, and it is the stance of technical neutrality which defines this attitude.

What, then, do we mean when we speak of the stance of technical neutrality? A brief digression at this point will help us place the concept of neutrality within its proper context. It is, perhaps, an unfortunate fact in the history of psychoanalytic ideas that Freud (1915) linked the concept of neutrality so closely with the "abstinence principle." By this linkage, Freud actually obscured the essential distinction between the way the analyst listens to and understands the patient's productions (i.e., an intrapsychic process) and a prescription for appropriate analytic response to such productions (i.e., an interpersonal behavior). By failing to maintain this distinction, Freud actually encouraged a situation in which the issue of nongratification of the patient's transferential wishes (i.e., the therapist's interpersonal response) overshadowed the equally important issue of the essential intrapsychic attitude toward what the patient was demanding (i.e., the neutral stance). In so doing, he also inadvertantly encouraged a situation in which the stance of neutrality became equated with a cold, distant, and perhaps even haughty analytic attitude. Thus analytic neutrality was seemingly obtained at the cost of one's basic tact and appropriateness in human relationships. That this was certainly not Freud's intention has been recently documented by Lipton (1977), as well as by Gill (1982).

Anna Freud (1954) attempted to refocus the concept of technical neutrality on the analytic stance by defining the analyst's position as lying equidistant from id, ego, and superego. In this perspective on the analyst's position vis-à-vis the patient's struggles, we see an effort to define the neutral stance as one of even-handed attention to the various components of psychic conflict, with the analyst not taking sides, so to speak. A relatively nonjudgmental attitude toward the various forces involved in conflict, and a focus on encouraging a similar attitude in the patient's own experience of his struggle, is highlighted here, with the essential task being one of increased objectivity and intellectual curiosity about the nature of one's own psychic distress. Brenner (1976) most articulately describes such an approach when he states:

> The very effectiveness of the therapy depends on the analyst's maintaining an analytic attitude, i.e., on his being nothing more and nothing less than an analyst, on his being guided consistently by the aim of helping his patient toward the goal of understanding the conflicts that give rise to his difficulties with the expectation that when he does understand them, the difficulties they have caused will diminish substantially or disappear (p. 109).

Whereas the admonition to be "nothing more and nothing less than an analyst" clearly implies the abstinence principle, here the emphasis is placed on the "analyzing function" (Rangell, 1969) of the analyst rather than on the issue of nongratification. Gill (1982) echos this view when he suggests that:

> Neutrality does not mean the avoidance of doing anything; but rather giving equal attention to all the patient's productions, without prior weighting

of one kind of material over another, and confining oneself to the analytic task, that is, abstaining from deliberate suggestion (p. 63).

Surely, in the clinical situation, the neutral stance most often involves abstinence with respect to gratifying transference wishes. But it is not invariably the case that such a combined stance can be maintained.[1] The importance of the distinction we are insisting on lies in the fact that a technically neutral stance enables the clinician to evaluate objectively whether or not it is clinically feasible to pursue his analyzing function at any particular time. More importantly, it enables him to make this judgment in a technically neutral rather than countertransferential way. Thus, from our perspective, technical neutrality can be maintained as an intrapsychic state, despite a breach in maintaining the interpersonal response of abstinence.

We have already indicated that it is on the analyst's specific technical stance, and not his personal idiosyncratic style, that the concept of neutrality rests. As a principle of technique, neutrality includes, as Rangell (1969) already indicated, "the analyst's objective and analyzing function" (p. 72). It is an intrapsychic attitude which addresses itself to the understanding of the deeper meanings of the patient's productions, without the implied behavioral connotations of coldness, remoteness, or arrogance. But, to say simply that the technically neutral stance of the analyst entails adherence to objective analysis of the patient's productions still does not inform us about the unique characteristics of this intrapsychic attitude which enables the analyst to hear and understand what needs to be analyzed. Thus the unique characteristics of the objective analyzing function require further elaboration.

Stone (1961) has provided us with an important conception of the analytic situation that may be helpful in clarifying the intrapsychic state that constitutes technical neutrality. Stone has suggested the concept of "intimate separation" to capture the unique qualities of the relationship between patient and analyst. Intimate separation implies a situation in which regressive re-fusions of self and object representations are balanced by a reflective awareness of the inescapable separateness of the partners to the dialogue. Thus analytic work requires a particular state, in both patient and analyst, in which there occurs oscillations between internal fantasy and a reflective awareness of

---

[1] An important example of such a situation, which occurred in the present case, will be discussed below. What effect the gratification of this patient's transference wish had on the evolving transference is an important issue, but one that is different from the conceptual distinction we are making here. The study of such occurrences is important and can be researched.

reality (Grand, 1983). It is a state that is negotiated across the "psychobiological bridge" of language, through which the inner world of the patient is conveyed to and empathically understood by the analyst. It is across this bridge that the analyzing function is joined in both patient and analyst. Indeed, it is primarily through the analyst's intense and empathic relatedness to what the patient says that the objective analyzing function operates.

Reik (1952) has termed such intense and empathic relatedness as "listening with the third ear"—a form of poised listening which requires a continuous oscillation or shifting between an openness and readiness to hear whatever the patient is telling us, and a more focused and directed attention to restructuring what has been heard. It is a state of consciousness that is notable by its capacity for surprise, that is, a readiness to hear the unexpected. Freedman, Barroso, Bucci, and Grand (1978) have documented such a process in therapeutic listening, and Freedman (1983) has characterized such listening as sequential rhythmic alternation between receiving and restructuring. He suggests that the:

> phase of receiving involves an openness to the intent of the other out there, a tolerance for multiple alternatives, and it involves an emphasis on subjectivity, that is, a suspension of the need to objectify or symbolize. The phase of restructuring involves a narrowing of attention, a reduction of possibilities aiming toward consolidation and synthesis, and an emphasis on objectification and symbolic representation. Only when both phases are activated in rhythmic sequence can optimal listening be said to occur (p. 409).

It is this stance, we suggest, of alternately suspending the need to objectify or symbolize on the one hand, and consolidating and synthesizing on the other, that defines technical neutrality. It is the analyst's capacity to listen with the third ear—the readiness for surprise and the oscillation between receiving and restructuring—that comprises the unique characteristics of the neutral analytic attitude. It is this special state of analytic consciousness, an acute attunement to the patient's productions, which underlies the analyst's relative objectivity in the performance of the analyzing function. In such a sequentially alternating state, the analyst oscillates between receiving what is said and restructuring it for the patient in ways that bring new meaning and organization to the experience.

In light of the above considerations, we may now return to consider how the therapeutic stance observed in the present case differs from the active stance observed in most forms of dynamic brief psychotherapy. Clearly, the most prominent aspect of the active treatment approach is its heavy emphasis on establishing the focus of work early in the treatment course. Forceful pressing of the patient to link contemporary dynamic issues with numerous genetic reconstructions forms the core of the work and is the basis for its being considered a manipulative type of treatment. A central feature of this emphasis on the early establishment of the focus is the necessity to select, from the patient's initial presentation of the problem, a key issue that the therapist defines as the one to be addressed. In so doing, the therapist must actively establish what is relevant and what is not, must objectify and symbolize with relatively little time for evenly suspended attention to receive what the patient says, and must withhold the capacity for surprise, because to be surprised may interfere with the rapid organization of a key issue that must be established as the focus. In short, the active therapist must restrict the oscillation between receiving and restructuring. A state of consciousness characterized by a narrowness of attention and a reduction of possibilities must be established, and the therapist must aim directly toward consolidation and synthesis, objectification and symbolic representation. It is this process of "prior weighting of one kind of material over another" (Gill, 1982) that forms the essential distinction between a manipulative stance and an analytically neutral one. What we wish to underscore about the therapeutic stance taken in the present treatment is that it was a stance that did give relatively more attention to all the patient's productions. It was a stance in which the therapist allowed the multiple alternatives of these productions to emerge, and in which a readiness for surprise was tolerated. It was one in which the need to objectify and symbolize was suspended for major portions of the brief treatment. In short, it was a relatively neutral, as opposed to an active manipulative, stance which distinguished this treatment from other brief psychotherapies, and, as such, it was one in which regression was tolerated with apparently little risk encountered for interminable treatment.

In this case, the therapist functioned within a classic analytic mode, with questions and clarifications being the primary interventions, and confrontations and interpretations used sparingly at points of negative transference resistance. These interventions all occurred within what Freud (1913) termed a climate of "sympathetic understanding," a climate that we are now able to term "analytic neutrality." For the most part, it was unnecessary for the therapist to act in ways other than what was required in order to function analytically. This suggests to us that, in large measure, the current emphasis of those espousing the necessity for special techniques for establishing and maintaining the "therapeutic alliance" (Gitelson, 1962; Greenson, 1966; Zetzel, 1966) is based on the conceptual confusion between the intrapsychic stance of technical neutrality and the interpersonal response of "abstinence." We agree with Brenner (1976) when he suggests that therapy depends on the analyst's maintaining an analytic attitude as long as "being nothing more and nothing less than an analyst" is understood to mean that the analyst functions on the basis of an intrapsychic state that oscillates between receiving and restructuring the patient's productions. Such a state does not preclude lapses of the principle of abstinence necessitated by the clinical exigencies of particular moments in any treatment. What it does require, however, is that such lapses be recognized and subjected to analytic scrutiny (Eissler, 1953).

The neutral stance of the therapist in the present case was marred by the introduction of only one modification of classic technique. It was at the conclusion of session 9, after the patient had undergone an intense and extremely upsetting regressive experience in relation to the transferential demand for caretaking from a castrating and powerful father–analyst, that the therapist offered the patient a glass of water and conveyed his concern about the patient's emotional state. Although only a minor divergence, which was justified by the patient's actual clinical state, it does precede and perhaps herald the subsequent shift in the patient's transference during session 10. The fearful, negative, and hostile relation to the therapist, characteristic of the previous three sessions, now alters in the direction of one in which the patient begins to distance himself from the therapist in anticipation of the rapidly approaching termination date. Although it is not possible, at this stage of our research, to determine to what degree this unanalyzed parameter of the treatment altered the transference, or to distinguish the effect of the parameter from the effect of the time-limit itself, it clearly represents a divergence from the neutral stance that ideally should have been analyzed and understood by both patient and therapist. The potentially manipulative effect of such a transference gratification underscores the need for a conceptualization of the analytic stance prior to the undertaking of systematic study of brief psychotherapy. Without such conceptualization, study of the transference as a process would be confounded by the effects of the manipulation. Given our goal of establishing a process that would be a microscopic version of the classic process, the manipulative character of the transference gratification offered by the therapist at the conclusion of session 9 will require careful scrutiny in the next phase of this research.

In consideration of the issues posed in this section, we would like to suggest that technical neutrality is the essential ingredient for any treatment that claims to be psychoanalytic. Not only does it establish the analytic situation as a unique form of dialogue, but it also establishes the central value inherent in the analytic process. We believe Gill (1982) is correct when he indicates that it is the therapist's task to teach the patient that the "crucial technique of analysis is to find . . . latent meaning" (p. 66). We suggest that the best method for the patient to understand this principle is the therapist's adherence to technical neutrality in the face of transference demands. Coercion, whether through aggressive authority or love, is a poor climate for learning.

THERAPEUTIC FOCUS

The establishment of therapeutic focus is, in our view, closely associated with the therapeutic stance of technical neutrality. In the following discussion, we will give consideration to some of the theoretical issues and technical strategies that governed the establishment of a therapeutic focus in the present case. Although we do not claim that the therapist was explicitly and consistently guided by the precepts we formulated here, we nevertheless feel that his approach to the establishment of focus is largely consistent with these ideas.[2]

Establishing the Focus

To say that a therapy is short-term is synonymous with saying that it has a focus. Particularly with respect to brief psychotherapy, the therapist is confronted with choices not only of which conflict to address and which to leave aside (i.e., how encompassing the therapy should be), but also choices of how "deeply" to address any particular conflict at any particular time. Considering both the importance and centrality of focus in brief psychotherapy, the questions of how one chooses a focus and defines the appropriate depth of intervention have neither been comprehensively nor, to our mind, satisfactorily addressed in the current literature on brief psychotherapy (for example, see Wallerstein, 1983).

Several brief psychotherapists have attempted to solve, or rather

---

[2]To some extent, it was only after treatment was completed and the case and its related issues were discussed that it became clear to us how indispensible it is to articulate and specify the ideas discussed here. While generally agreed on formulations might suffice for long-term clinical treatment, they are grossly insufficient for brief psychotherapeutic work.

preempt, these problems by designating a focus a priori, that is, selecting and directing the treatment along the lines of certain predetermined universal psychodynamic themes (e.g., the struggle of over-dependency and separation, or specific triangular oedipal conflicts). But, as we have suggested earlier, such predetermination of focus inevitably runs the risk of artifically maximizing an attitude in the patient based more on the therapist's assumptions than on what is actually central to the patient's own pathology. Particularly since the effort of these therapies is to establish the definitive focus in the first few sessions, therapeutic work may not be as powerfully related to the patient's core conflicts as these emerge later in the treatment. For example, from the way our patient presented himself in the initial sessions, a focus could have easily been construed within either of the above-mentioned universal themes. But this would not necessarily have made either of these foci the best possible formulation for this particular patient, nor have led to the most productive approach to his conflicts. In our own approach, the therapist did not assume a preference for dealing with any particular conflict, but rather he attempted to achieve the *maximum* that this patient's current conflicts, relationships, ego strength, and ongoing transferential dynamics would allow. Thus the therapist assumed a technically neutral stance with respect to the therapeutic focus, which then allowed a more internally generated and consistent focus to emerge within the patient in the ongoing transferential relationship.

How is this approach different from the generally accepted approaches formulated by current brief psychotherapies? Davanloo (1978), for example, stresses that "from the very first interview" he uses the past–present transference link:

> setting up a link between the contemporary pattern of the patient's behavior with significant people in his present life with the vertical, the genetic pattern of the patient's behavior with parents or parent substitutes, and further linking it with the transference pattern (p. 344).

Although this formulation is cogent and consistent with certain psychoanalytic conceptualizations of transference analysis (e.g., see Gill, 1982), it is difficult to see how such rapid interpretive work could be accepted by a patient, nor how the patient could develop a sense of conviction that it was so. While the patient may not develop conviction, he/she may accept the early interpretation on the strength of the therapist's authority or on a rapid attachment to the therapist. But, from our perspective, such acceptance is a suggestive effect and surely must result in a distortion of the transference in ways discussed earlier. Given the brevity of the therapeutic course, little opportunity would be available for such transference distortions to be analyzed and worked through.[3]

In our own approach, the therapist allows the transference to emerge and develop in as natural way as is possible within the time-limits of the treatment course. As the transference develops and intensifies, it serves as a prism for formulating the patient's core conflicts and the focus of the therapy. Thus, insofar as transference takes time to crystalize, the focus and goals of the therapy may not be as precisely formulated at the beginning of treatment as has been suggested it should be by Davanloo and his colleagues. Rather than impose a focus from without, and artificially manipulate the transference relationship, our approach awaited the development of a transference relationship which, itself, defined the focus. It is for this reason that technical neutrality is crucially related to the establishment of a focus in our work.

Whereas our patient began his therapy quite motivated for treatment and with an essentially positive transference, it took several sessions for him to crystalize a set of attitudes toward the therapist which had definite transferential features. In the first two sessions, he was evasive, playing a sort of hide-and-seek game with the therapist—revealing highly charged conflicts only to gloss over them quickly. A fuller meaning of this behavior became clearer only in sessions 3 and 4, where the patient yearned for the therapist to take him by the hand and tell him what to do and what not to do. These cloaked transference wishes were accompanied by equally disguised fears of being taken advantage of, both sexually and financially. When the therapist did not respond to those wishes in the way the patient had hoped he would, resistances, in the form of latenesses and complaints about people who are slow, emerged in sessions 5 and 6. The patient blamed "them" for his not achieving more in his life.

All of these developments in the transference offer the best clues for understanding the patient's extratransference relationships—with his wife, daughter, clients, former therapist, father, mother, and so on. They help us understand why the solutions he proposes for himself (i.e., to become more aggressive) do not quite work. The depth of his yearnings for submissiveness and the easy arousability of his aggressive impulses come to be strongly expressed in the unfolding transference which is, in a sense, the final arbiter in choosing the focus.

---

[3] See Footnote 3, Chapter 3 for a fuller discussion of this problem in relation to Gill's (1982) distinction between analysis of the resistance to the awareness of transference and analysis of the resistance to the resolution of transference.

Working Through the Focus

The state of the transference is equally important in guiding interpretive work once the focus has been clearly established. It is the state of the transference that best reveals the extent to which the focus has been, or is likely to be, worked through. If, for example, the patient denies the wish to continue work with the therapist, in session 11, after having threatened in session 9 to kill himself if treatment stops, we have useful information that helps us qualify our understanding of his supposedly final decision to proceed with a divorce from his wife. Or, if he must still either viciously attack the therapist or unconditionally submit to him, and cannot yet fully appreciate or transcend this dichotomy, how can he be expected to understand the interpretation of such feelings about his father?

In any therapy, some issues appear to be easier to approach outside the transference, whereas others are readily approachable within the transference. This results in a certain spread or tension in the patient's experience with respect to the level of his adaptedness or maturity vis-à-vis the therapist. This tension between the levels of adaptation both within and outside the transference is what Loewald (1960) has designated the motivation for change in treatment. It provides an opportunity to work through the core conflict further as the patient strives to "close the gap" in the transference. In short-term, time-limited therapy, however, there is little time for such continuing and ever-more successful working through. Therefore, we are tempted to suggest that, in order to maximize the efficiency of the therapeutic work in brief treatments, the therapist should not attempt to achieve solutions to conflicts outside the transference at levels beyond which the patient has been able to achieve in the transference edition of his conflict. For instance, "hammering in" an interpretation about the patient's homosexual tendencies toward various men to whom he happens to become attached will have little chance of being constructively integrated by the patient if he has consistently declined to own up to such feelings in the transference.[4] To repeat, the current state of the transference is the best indicator of which extratransference interpretations the patient is likely to accept on more than a purely intellectual level.

In summary, we have presented, in this chapter, our view of the unique characteristics of the present treatment approach, which dis-

---

[4]This does not mean that, in the present instance, the therapist might not have encouraged P. to talk more about his homosexuality, or that this issue might not have been more forcefully and usefully addressed both in and out of the transference.

tinguish it from other short-term therapies. Both the concepts of technical neutrality and therapeutic focus in brief psychotherapy have been reevaluated and amplified in respect to their implications for the systematic development, intensification, and working through of the transference. We have suggested that a technically neutral stance, distinct from the principle of abstinence, permits the emergence and coalescing of a specific prototypic relationship theme, which then defines the focus of the analytic working through of the transference. In the final chapter, we will discuss the implications such a view has for the study of brief psychotherapy, and specifically suggest how such a model may be useful for studying the psychoanalytic process.

8 Conclusion

It was our intention in this study to show that, by carefully organizing a treatment along the classical lines of therapeutic neutrality and non-manipulated focus, a process analagous to a psychoanalytic transference neurosis could be elicited and partially resolved within the time-limits of a brief psychotherapy. It was our hope that if such a process could be organized in this relatively short-term treatment, it could provide a research model for the study of transference, as well as other important process variables intrinsic to psychoanalytic work, which are so difficult to study in the natural setting of the classic psychoanalytic situation.

To the extent that a significant transference paradigm did emerge in the present case, did intensify into a process that bore the characteristics of a transference neurosis, and, most importantly, did lead to some degree of structural reorganization through the partial working through of this "transference neurosis," we feel that the purposes and goals of our present work have been accomplished and a more formal study of transference in this brief psychotherapy can be undertaken. However, having established, through the methods of group consensus and converging data, a sense of conviction that a neutral therapeutic stance entailing relatively little active focusing on the part of the therapist could elicit and consolidate a transference paradigm, what relevance do our findings have for brief psychotherapy more generally? Specifically, what sorts of issues are raised by our clinical study in regard to current understanding of the process of short-term dynamic psychotherapy?

IMPLICATIONS FOR THE STUDY OF BRIEF
PSYCHOTHERAPY

We would like to highlight several issues that have become more focused in our own minds as a result of our work with this case. First, we would like to address the question of whether or not regression can be tolerated in brief treatment approaches because this issue underlies much of the rationale for managing the transference in brief psychotherapies. It also underlies the distinction between the more classical approach that we have taken in our own work and the major brief treatment approaches currently available.

As we indicated earlier, there has been a strong tendency, in the current brief psychotherapies, to inhibit the process of regression actively through the manipulation of the transference relationship. The rationale for such active focusing of the treatment relationship has been based on the widespread assumption that regression, in short-term treatment, is inimical to the goals of such treatment and would lead to an interminable therapeutic relationship through the encouragement of strong dependency feelings in the patient. Moreover, it has been assumed that limiting regression, through actively focusing the patient's feelings away from the therapist and onto their original genetic targets, ensures immediacy and real affect without the disruptive effects that occur with the appearance of a crystallized transference neurosis.

The course of the treatment in the present case provides evidence that does not support these assumptions. Not only was it possible to work through the patient's significant passive, dependent longings for the "good father" of the positive transference, but even the enormous rage and helplessness of the crystallized, predominantly negative transference neurosis gave way to more benign and grateful feelings toward the therapist as treatment rapidly drew to a close. The neutral stance led to neither interminable treatment nor overly disruptive effects in the patient's life.

Earlier, we discussed the possibility that the time-limit itself serves as a limiting condition for the iatrogenic regressive process. Thus knowledge of the end point actually limits the depth to which a patient will go in reexperiencing core conflicts. In light of this fact, it seems to us all the more important to allow regression to occur. Without such regression, a crystallized transference paradigm could not be experienced nor worked through. Our work with the present patient demonstrated to us that, at least for certain cases, adherence to therapeutic neutrality and nonmanipulative focusing does elicit a crystallized transference paradigm with little danger of a malignant regression.

Whatever disruptive effects did occur here, they were surely a small price to pay for the depth of conviction and understanding that became available for our patient as a result of his regressive experiences and their working through.

It is not so clear to us that had we rapidly juxtaposed the genetic material with transference interpretations, in the absence of a crystallized transference paradigm, we would have achieved the sort of mutative effect which current brief psychotherapists claim. Rather, it seems to us for reasons already suggested, that such a process could have only addressed the resistance to the awareness of transference rather than the resistance to the resolution of the transference. As such, it might have resulted in intellectual understanding rather than the kind of deep conviction that we feel the present patient attained from the intense emotional turmoil of the middle phase of his treatment.

In light of these considerations, it is clear to us that brief treatments, which actively interpret transference manifestations prior to the consolidation of a more developed transference paradigm, limit the depth of conviction that can be attained from working through these interpretations. From our perspective, then, the crucial distinction between our more classic approach to the analysis of the transference and the approaches proposed by most current brief psychotherapists lies in the fact that we do not limit the regressive development of the transference paradigm, and indeed, await this development before attempting its systematic interpretation.

Thus one by-product of our effort to research the psychoanalytic concept of transference through the use of the brief psychotherapy model is that we have been able to establish the feasibility and efficacy of a more psychoanalytically consistent model of brief psychotherapy than those active forms of brief psychotherapy currently being utilized. This is not to say, however, that we would favor the present form of treatment as a substitute for classical treatment when such is possible and indicated. Our clinical summary of this case suggested that the patient, possibly for the first time in his life, began to question and air some of his psychological mechanisms as a result of the treatment, and that a new equilibrium began to emerge in which he experienced himself as a sadder, less inflated, but freer and less burdened man. The brevity of the treatment, however, did not permit complete working through. Under the influence of termination, the patient felt even more of a need to rely on his most proven defenses. Thus, despite some new alignments in his psyche, the more primitive elements remained prominent to the end, along with fragile, new, more adaptive elements. The psychological test data provided converging validation of these new alignments in the patient's psyche, and also revealed the primitive elements which remained unresolved. Thus it was clear to us that the patient studied here could certainly have benefited from a long-term treatment conducted along the classical lines of the psychoanalytic situation. The fragility of the structural reorganization documented, in this case, speaks strongly for the advisability of a more intense, long-term relationship for patients such as ours. The follow-up testing 8 months after the termination of treatment highlighted this fragility as we witnessed the return of depressive and paranoid ideation and the longing for renewed contact with the "good father" of the positive transference relationship. It was clear to us throughout the treatment that more solid structural rearrangements could certainly not be counted on in a treatment period as short as was ours. While the gains in the area of a more realistic appraisal of reality (i.e., "the sadder but less burdened man") did seem stable, overall there was a tendency on the part of this patient to maintain the stability of his current adjustments through the continued resort to relatively maladaptive defensive maneuvers (e.g., regressive acting out).

This brings us to the second issue raised by our study, that is, the clinical efficacy of short-term therapies, particularly with respect to what Winokur et al. (1981) have posed as their "formidable challenge [of brief psychotherapies] to long-term analytic therapists" (p. 127). In our admittedly brief experience with short-term therapy, we have come both to respect its possibilities as well as to question more seriously the intent of those who seem to speak for the general utility of such treatment forms. Although the results of our single case cannot, of course, stand alone, our intense involvement in trying to understand this case has provided us with some sense of the clinical limitations of brief psychotherapy. While the possibility exists that our particular form of transference-focused, neutral, brief psychotherapy might not have been as therapeutically productive as the more active, manipulative forms of brief treatment, we still doubt that any form of treatment which artificially limits the natural course of the transference neurosis and its working-through process will provide a patient with a therapeutic yield as deep, as rich, and as complete as that attainable through long-term treatment.

Clinically, then, we do not feel justified in extending our work with this patient into a formal treatment model. It is our impression that brief psychotherapists have overstated the generality of their work and extended their enthusiasm for this form of treatment altogether too far ahead of their own clinical findings in their rush for general clinical applicability. As was suggested by Wallerstein (1983), the "evangelic" and "charismatic" nature of the current movement only obscures some of the more important questions concerning the nature of follow-up data, and the processes responsible for clinical change. More sophisticated techniques for evaluating the process of brief psychotherapy are needed.

This latter point raises the third issue we would like to address: the current reliance on symptom reduction as a measure of success of treatment, and the inadequacy of clinical outcome as a validator of the therapeutic process. As was suggested earlier, whereas these issues are a problem for the field of psychotherapy generally, they are a far more crucial problem for the brief psychotherapies because of their tendency to manipulate the transference relationship actively. How these active manipulations become internalized or integrated into the patient's mental experience is extremely important when attempts are made to assess the outcome of brief treatments.

The current reliance on symptom reduction as a measure of the success of treatment, while adequate from a national mental health perspective, does not provide evidence for the validity of the claims for "complete success" that have been asserted in the brief psychotherapy literature. To assert global improvement on the basis of symptom reduction tells us little about either structural reorganization or the process by which it occurs. Our own experience with P. is a case in point. From the perspective of symptom reduction, we might have considered the outcome of this case to have been an extremely successful one. After all, the condition that brought P. to treatment (i.e., the mycardial infarction) was no longer producing severe anxiety, and his depressive feelings and nihilistic attitudes seemed to have lifted sufficiently at the end of treatment so that he now could assert that he no longer felt the need for further treatment. Even the upsurge of suicidal feelings 8 months following termination were very short-lived, giving way rapidly to the therapist's interventions in the follow-up interview.

To view this patient's outcome in this way, however, totally overlooks the fragility of the structural reorganization that has occurred, the continued resort to his former proven defenses, and the intractibility of his primitive depressive and paranoid longing for the "good father" of the positive transference. Although our patient's progress, in respect to his clearer vision of reality, was certainly a major indicator of change, it would be quite misleading for us to suggest that this represented a relatively stable structural reorganization of the patient's mental life. What we can say, however, is that, given an optimal set of environmental circumstances, this fragile new organization would have a high probability of stabilizing. If such stabilization does occur, we could then expect less of a need for the use of defensive acting out, and a reduction in the passive longing for the protective and loving father of the positive transference. Thus it is only from the perspective of a clear view of the way the treatment process affected the patient's transferential involvement with his therapist that probabalistic statements can be made about treatment outcome. Outcome, in this sense, is based on a close inspection of the forms and transformations that have occurred in the patient's transferential relationship to his therapist. These forms and transformations of the transference enable us to specify those aspects of the patient's pathology which have been significantly touched by the treatment process, and they also enable us to specify the extent to which those and other aspects of the patient's pathology still require further work.

Measures of global improvement and measurs of symptom reduction, even if carefully predicted on the basis of initial formulations of the patient's "basic neurotic conflict" (Malan, 1963), fail to provide links between therapeutic outcomes and the processes responsible for them. Ultimately, it is the processes responsible for therapeutic change that require specification in order that we can evaluate the utility of any treatment form. Data linking outcome variables to such processes would provide some measure of validity to claims of success by various treatment modalities. It is through such relationships that progress in the study of therapeutic efficacy will eventually be attained. Data linking specific interventions to change in specific patterns of psychological organization would be a first step toward addressing these issues. Although the present phase of this study was not designed to consider issues of change in response to therapeutic intervention, it does provide the data on which such a study could be undertaken.

PROSPECTS FOR FUTURE RESEARCH

Insofar as short-term psychotherapy can be made to mirror (even if only in a somewhat limited way), the processes that occur in long-term psychoanalytic treatment, it offers a unique mode for studying such processes. In this monograph of P.'s 14-session therapy, we feel that we have established, through the process of documented clinical consensus, that a crystallized transference paradigm did emerge, and that the treatment process can be meaningfully understood from the perspective of the emergence, intensification, and partial working through of this transference paradigm.

Given the fact that this first stage of our study of P. has resulted in a sense of clinical conviction that a transference paradigm did occur, we are now prepared to move ahead to the second phase of our research study. As we suggested earlier, the phase of experimentation proper will entail the operationalizing of the concept of transference and the study of the covariation of this process with other variables of interest. Thus the next phase of our research will be concerned with the systematic and quantitative study of the transference.

The application of any quantitative measure to a case that has been so intensely studied from a clinical perspective has the unique advantage that we will be in a position to assess both the meaningfulness of our clinical understanding as well as the comprehensiveness of the measuring instrument. In this way, blind spots with respect to our clinical understanding as well as deficiencies in the measuring instrument can be brought into bold relief. This is especially important since the main fruits of quantitative psychoanalytic research will derive from advances in quantitative methods (Luborsky & Spence, 1978) that are valid indicators of clinical phenomena.

Systematic quantitative research on psychoanalytic treatment is still relatively rare and, up to recently, has been somewhat divorced from the theoretical and technical advances in our field. The recent development of a method for analyzing aspects of the patient's experience of the therapeutic relationship (Gill & Hoffman, 1982) is the first attempt by a noted psychoanalytic theoretician to devise a quantitative research tool. We view this as a signal achievement in that it represents a sophisticated response to a need articulated by Luborsky and Spence (1978), who state that "despite its rather prosaic nature, a systematic naturalistic inventory of the analytic process is long overdue" (p. 361).

As a first step in our own efforts to quantify the phenomena of transference in our brief psychotherapy case, we plan to apply both Gill and Hoffman's (1982) system for scoring transference manifestations in psychotherapy sessions, and Luborsky's (1977) method for scoring the "core relationship theme" to the clinical data of our treatment sessions. These systems provide, first, a way of operationalizing the concept of transference so that we may quantify the emergent transference paradigm, and second, a way of defining a focus in these treatment sessions, as reflected in the evocation of the core relationship theme. Comparisons between these two measures should help us to understand the relationship between transference, as an emergent process, and the establishment of focus in this brief psychotherapy. However, the comparison of these measures with the clinical understanding of the case that emerged in this monograph should enable us to assess the degree to which either of these quantitative measures reflect this clinical understanding.

Finally, although both Gill and Hoffman's method and Luborsky's method are related to the concept of transference, they each measure different aspects of it. Gill and Hoffman's method relates specifically to the awareness of the transference, whereas Luborsky's system taps a more general aspect of transference, possibly even something more encompassing than transference, that is, "the main unconscious fantasy," as suggested by Arlow (1977). Thus the comparison of these two approaches to analyzing the therapeutic interaction should, we hope, contribute to a more systematic understanding of how transference can manifest itself in the context of analytic work.

In conclusion, we are mindful of the fact that critics of single-case research might bemoan the large expenditure of both time and effort entailed in the study of one patient. After all, the accumulation of a large data base on a single case does have limited generalizability to the psychotherapy population at large. In response to such critics, we can only say that, in light of the current state of the field of psychotherapy research, a field burdened by methodological problems of enormous difficulty as well as by theoretical confusions, the intensive and carefully documented study of single cases may provide a timeworn alternative which was, after all, the clinical method of choice of our forebearers. From our own perspective, it may be a far better choice to know a great deal about a limited number of people, than to know relatively little about many.

REFERENCES

Alexander, F., & French, T. M. (1946) *Psychoanalytic therapy.* New York: Ronald Press.

Arlow, J. A. (1977). Discussion of issues posed in section 6 of *Communicative Structures and Psychic Structures.* In N. Freedman & S. Grand (Eds.), *Communicative structures and psychic structures: a psychoanalytic interpretation of communication* (pp. 441–450). New York: Plenum Press.

Bird, B. (1972). Notes on transference: universal phenomenon and the hardest part of analysis. *Journal of the American Psychoanalytic Association, 20,* 267–301.

Brenner, C. (1976). *Psychoanalytic technique and psychic conflict.* New York: International Universities Press.

Brenner, C. (1979). Working alliance, therapeutic alliance and transference. *Journal of the American Psychoanalytic Association, 27* (Suppl.), 137–157.

Brenner, C. (1982). *The mind in conflict.* New York: International Universities Press.

Dahl, H. (1972). A quantitative study of psychoanalysis. In R. R. Holt & E. Peterfreund (Eds.), *Psychoanalysis and contemporary science,* (pp. 237–257). New York: Mac-Millan.

Dahl, H. (1974). The measurement of meaning in psychoanalysis by computer analysis of verbal contexts. *Journal of the American Psychoanalytic Association, 22,* 37–57.

Davanloo, H. (ed.) (1978). *Basic principles and techniques in short term dynamic psychotherapy.* New York: S.P. Medical & Scientific Books.

Deutch, R., & Murphy, W. F. (1955). *The clinical interview.* New York: International Universities Press.

Eissler, K. (1953). The effect of the structure of the ego on psychoanalytic technique. *Journal of the American Psychological Association, 1,* 104–143.

Ferenczi, S. (1920). The further development of an active therapy in psychoanalysis. In *Further contributions to the theory and technique of psychoanalysis* (pp. 198–217). London: Hogarth Press, 1950.

Ferenczi, S., & Rank, O. (1925). *The development of psychoanalysis.* New York: Nervous & Mental Disease Publishing.

Flegenheimer, W. V. (1982). *Techniques of brief psychotherapy.* New York: Jason Aronson.

Freedman, N. (1983). On psychoanalytic listening: the construction, paralysis, and reconstruction of meaning. *Psychoanalysis and Contemporary Thought, 6,* 405–434.

Freedman, N., Barroso, F., Bucci, W., & Grand, S. (1978). The bodily manifestations of listening. *Psychoanalysis and Contemporary Thought, 1,* 187–194.

Freud, A. (1954). Problems of technique in adult analysis. *Bulletin of the Philadelphia Association, 4,* 44–69.

Freud, S. (1895). *Studies on hysteria, S.E., 2,* 1–309.

Freud, S. (1905). Fragment of an analysis of a case of hysteria. *S.E., 7,* 7–122.

Freud, S. (1912). The dynamics of transference. *S.E., 12,* 99–108.

Freud, S. (1913). On beginning the treatment (further recommendations on the technique of psychoanalysis I). *S.E., 12,* 123–144.

Freud, S. (1915) Observations on Transferred Love, *S.E., 12,* 159–171.

Freud, S. (1916–1917). Introductory lectures on psychoanalysis. *S.E., 15 & 16,* 243–496.

Freud, S. (1918). From the history of an infantile neurosis. *S.E., 17,* 7–122.

Freud, S. (1920). Beyond the pleasure principle. *S.E., 18,* 7–64.

Freud, S. (1925). An autobiographical study. *S.E., 20,* 7–74.

Freud, S. (1926). The question of lay analysis. *S.E., 20,* 183–258.

Freud, S. (1933). New introductory lectures on psychoanalysis. *S.E., 22,* 5–182.

Freud, S. (1937). Analysis terminable and interminable. *S.E., 23,* 216–253.

Freud, S. (1940). An outline of psychoanalysis. *S.E., 23,* 144–207.

Gill, M. (1982). *Analysis of transference: I, theory and technique.* New York: International Universities Press.

Gill, M. & Hoffman, I. Z. (1982). *Analysis of Transference: II, Studies of Nine Audio-Recorded Psychoanalytic Sessions.* New York: International Universities Press.

Gitelson, M. (1962). The curative factors in psychoanalysis. *International Journal of Psychoanalysis, 43,* 3–22.

Grand, S. (1983). Transference and the therapeutic alliance. *Issues in Ego Psychology, 5,* 11–18.

Greenson, R. R. (1966). Discussion. In R. E. Litman (ed.), *Psychoanalysis in the Americas* (pp. 131–132). New York: International Universities Press.

Harrower, M. (1958). *Personality change and development as measured by the projective techniques.* New York: Grune & Stratton.

Horowitz, M. (1977). Life event questionnaires for measuring presumptive stress. *Psychosomatic Medicine, 39,* 413–431.

Horowitz, M. (1979). Impact of event scale: a measure of subjective stress. *Psychosomatic medicine, 41,* 209–218.

Lipton, S. D. (1977). The advantages of Freud's technique as shown in his analysis of the Rat Man. *International Journal of Psychoanalysis, 58,* 255–274.

Loewald, H. (1960). On the therapeutic action of psychoanalysis. *International Journal of Psychoanalysis, 41,* 16–33.

Luborsky, L. (1977). Measuring a pervasive psychic structure in psychotherapy: The core conflictual relationship theme. In N. Freedman & S. Grand (Eds.), *Communicative structures and psychic structures: a psychoanalytic interpretation of communication* (pp. 367–395). New York: Plenum Press.

Luborsky, L., & Spence, D. (1978). Quantitative research on psychoanalytic theory. In S. Garfield & A. Bergin (Eds.), *Handbook of psychotherapy and behavior change.* New York: Wiley.

Malan, D. H. (1963). *A study of brief psychotherapy.* New York: Plenum Press.

Malan, D. H. (1976). *The frontier of brief psychotherapy: an example of the convergence of research and clinical practice.* New York: Plenum Press.

Mann, J. (1973). *Time limited psychotherapy.* Cambridge, MA: Harvard University Press.

Marmor, J. (1980). Historical roots. In H. Davanloo (Ed.), *Short term dynamic psychotherapy.* New York: Spectrum Publications.

Rangell, L. (1969). The intrapsychic process and its analysis. *International Journal of Psychoanalysis, 50,* 65–78.

Reik, T. *Listening with the third ear.* New York: Farrar, Straus & Company.

Rogawski, A. S. (1982). The current status of brief psychotherapy. *Bulletin of the Menninger Clinic, 46,* 331–351.

Sandler, J. (1983). Reflections on some relations between psychoanalytic concepts and psychoanalytic practice. *International Journal of Psychoanalysis, 64,* 35–45.

Schafer, R. (1955). Psychological test evaluation of personality change during intensive psychotherapy. *Projective testing and psychoanalysis: selected papers* (pp. 25–28). New York: International Universities Press, 1967.

Schafer, R. (1979). Character, ego syntonicity, and character change. *Journal of the American Psychoanalytic Association, 27,* 867–891.

Schwager, E., & Spear, W. (1981). New perspectives on psychological tests as measures of change. *Bulletin of the Menninger Clinic, 45,* 527–541.

Seitz, P. F. D. (1966). The consensus problem in psychoanalytic research. In L. Gottschalk & A. Auerbach (Eds.), *Methods of research in psychotherapy.* (pp. 209–225). New York: Appleton-Century-Crofts.

Sifneos, P. E. (1972). *Short-term psychotherapy and emotional crisis.* Cambridge, MA: Harvard University Press.

Sifneos, P. E. (1979). *Short term dynamic psychotherapy.* New York: Plenum Press.

Sobel, D. (1982). A new and controversial short-term psychotherapy. *The New York Times Sunday Magazine,* November 21.

Stekel, W. (1940). *Technique of analytical psychotherapy.* Eden Paul & Ceder Paul (Trans.). New York: Norton.

Stone, L. (1961). *The psychoanalytic situation.* New York: International Universities Press.

Wallerstein, R. S. (1963). The problem of the assessment of change in psychotherapy. *International Journal of Psychoanalysis, 44,* 31–41.

Wallerstein, R. S. (1966). The current state of psychotherapy: Theory, practice, research. *Journal of the American Psychoanalytic Association, 14,* 183–225.

Wallerstein, R. S. (1979). Review of *Toward the validation of dynamic psychotherapy* by David Malan. *Journal of the American Psychoanalytic Association, 27,* 275–279.

Wallerstein, R. S. (1983). Review of *Basic principles and techniques in dynamic short term psychotherapy* by H. Davanloo. *Journal of the American Psychoanalytic Association, 31,* 780–784.

Winokur, M., Messer, S. B., & Schacht, T. (1981). Contributions to the theory and practice of short-term dynamic psychotherapy. *Bulletin of the Menninger Clinic, 45,* 125–142.

Zetzel, E. (1966). The analytic situation. In R. E. Litman (Ed.), *Psychoanalysis in the Americas* (pp. 86–106). New York: International Universities Press.